Humanising Management:

Transformation through Human Values

Humanising Management:

Transformation through Human Values

G.P. Rao

Prof. (Retd.) IIM

Kolkata

Ane Books Pvt. Ltd.

New Delhi ♦ Chennai

Humanising Management: Transformation through Human Values

G.P. Rao

Price: ₹ 1495/-
Pages: 217 + xxvi

Published by

Ane Books Pvt. Ltd.

4821, Parwana Bhawan, 1st Floor, 24 Ansari Road, Darya Ganj,
New Delhi - 110 002, Tel.: +91(011) 23276843-44, Fax: +91(011) 23276863
e-mail: kapoor@anebooks.com, Website: www.anebooks.com

Branch Office:

- Avantika Niwas, 1st Floor, 19 Doraiswamy Road, T. Nagar,
  Chennai - 600 017, Tel.: +91(044) 28141554, 28141209
  e-mail: anebookschennai@gmail.com, rathinam@anebooks.com

ISBN : 978-93-8015-638-5

Printed at : Trident Enterprises, NOIDA.

Foreword
Three Perspectives

Management is a great work because it involves dealing with people and people need love and compassion. It is not enough to pay them; it is not enough to give them a job. It is something more than that. You need to have love and respect for the person working with you and for you – for that person is both your brother and your sister... Please love the people who are working for you for they are great people and they will love you in return .In your love that you gave them, they will give you their understanding. My prayer for you is: Love your people and that you love them until it hurts. You cannot love unless you know them, unless they are somebody to you. They are an individual, a man, a woman created for greater thing, a child of God – my brother, my sister, and if you could realize that then your management and your firm, whatever and wherever you are, will grow and bring much fruit.

— Mother Teresa: Address to Calcutta Management Association, Calcutta, 1979.

Foreword One

I cannot recall any decision in my personal or professional life which had only advantages and no disadvantages. The choice from the possible alternatives had to be based on a criteria that could provide a direction for choice of the particular alternative. Formal organisations where a large number of persons are required to take decisions have to articulate criteria that should guide their decision-choice. If this is not done the organisation is likely to greatly suffer from misunderstanding among people within the organisation and the public with which they deal. These criteria includes a value-base which is intended to give the organsiation a distinct identity.

Akio Morita of Sony Corporation fame in his book titled Made in Japan provides an interesting example of their belief system guiding a decision to turn down an order for supply of one million radios to one of the biggest retail chain stores at a time when they were promoting their new invention Walkman. They were a small company and needed finances and an order of that size would have solved many problems for them. The company believed in life-long engagement of employees, and Morita believed that they would have to add a number of employees to produce one million radios, and if they failed to get that size of repeat orders, they will be required to hold redundant labour force, the cost of that Sony cold not manage. The question of sending the redundant labour as companies do elsewhere was not an action-choice in view of their belief-system. This was one of the important reasons for not accepting a huge order that could have helped the company financially.

The concern for articulation and implementation of values has become critical for many reasons. Developments in science and technology provide knowledge-base that have offered solutions to heal illnesses, provide refined data for diagnosis, improved communications, improved agricultural and production processes and helped in many unaccounted ways. However, the same knowledge-base has generated instruments of destruction of mankind and society.

Religion provides solace to many people but the same scriptures are used to destabilize society and take human life. I believe the choice between using knowledge for good of society or to harm and destroy it rest on the values, faith, belief, and sentiments that people have. These attributes guide choices. They do not have to be part of a formal religion but they are something beyond 'self'. Some people may refer to these as spiritual part of self. Broadly this is the sense in which I believe spirituality is used in this book.

I have known Prof. G.P. Rao for more than forty years. He has devoted many years of his academic career in the study of values and their propagation in work organisations. An intervention plan requires a great deal of patience, time and effort. The people concerned have to consciously examine the desired values and operationalise them. They have to develop conviction of these among a large group of people so that they guide their choice at work and in life. Prof. Rao has evolved a method of articulating values and helping an organsiation to implement them. He refers to this as 3-D Process. This consists of diagnosis, discovery and development. Together with some actively interested persons in business and academia, he has set up an organisation called *Spandan*. Besides research, *Spandan* has the task of propagating values and providing service to implement these in organisations. This book describes the evolution of the idea and the nature of service that *Spandan* provides, and discusses the rationale of the model.

With expanding base of knowledge and developments in our capabilities to harness the unknown, it is apparent that value choice to guide right and wrong has become important. Furthermore this choice or the criteria has to lead to the wellbeing of the society and the quality of life of its members.

Many organisations have a set of values printed and hung on walls, or placed on work tables. A large number of studies have shown that the values in that list are hardly noticeable in the way work is done or in relationships within and outside the organisation. The intentions of management in preparing the list may be credit worthy but if these values are not reflected in the manner that work is carried out or as decisions-criteria throughout the organisation, the purpose that the management may have had in mind is unlikely to be served. Hence, the formulation of values and implementation of these is much more than a casual exercise of preparing a list of desired attributes. Some concerns in respect to identifying organisational values may be useful, some of which are discussed below.

The first concern which is often raised is whether value criteria improves the bottom line. In the long run it would be surprising if the value system fails to do so. However, the direct impact of identifying a value-base and its being guide to decision choice is likely to show up in conversion of skepticism among the people into hope, lack of faith in trust, sources of conflict and hostility into an effort to understand motives and exercise tolerance; and, many similar people related behaviour patterns. The outcome of the value-base would show on the faces of people, feeling of belongingness to the organisation and concerns for its wellbeing. Cumulatively these features of the work community may generate an urge to achieve better results but seeking direct one-to-one relationship between value system and the bottom line is likely to be a misplaced expectation.

Another concern is that articulation of values rarely differentiates social obligations from values that guide a decision choice. An example will illustrate the point. In a large number of organisations a list of values includes statements such as pay taxes or customer orientation. Paying taxes is a social obligation where non-payment is open to punitive action. In a society where payment of tax is voluntary, or does not lead to censure, perhaps tax paying can be seen as a value. In most societies this is considered as a social obligation. In the same way customer-orientation is a business imperative. Failure to do so has strong negative consequences. In a controlled market environment. Which often suffers from shortages of goods and services, customer care and orientation by an organisation can be seen as a value. In a competitive market situation neglect of customer is a road to self destruction. I mention these concerns to suggest that the process of identification of values needs conceptual clarity if they have to be vastly shared by employees as a decision-guide.

Whether all readers fully or partially agree with Prof. G.P. Rao's 3-D Process of value articulation and implementation, the concern for a decision-criteria for managements is unavoidable for their own wellbeing and that of the society that sustains them. I hope this book helps organisations to pause and think about the damages of not thinking about the issue.

New Delhi

— Prof. Ishwar Dayal
Former Director
Indian Institute of Management, Lucknow

Foreword Two

It is an empirical truism that the writing style reflects a writer's personality. Prof. Dr. Rao's book on *Humanising Management* bears good testimony to this truth. Mellowed by almost five decades of teaching experience and encounters with the wider society, the work builds up, with a mature and serene confidence, on the *rishi*-like 'belief', perhaps even faith, in the divinity and goodness of man (and woman to be sure). At a time when mammonization and robotization are on the verge of converting man fully to mere 'human resource', the bold call for humanisation of management is reassuring, though against the tide. It is gratifying too that the work begun at IIM-Calcutta (1978-79) for integrating Indian ethos and human values into management, is branching off in new directions through books like these by G.P. Rao and others.

The Mother-cum-Maternalistic disposition or ethos has been held out as the driving force behind the process of humanisation. In *sanatan* Indian ethos worship of divinity as Mother has always been a major route self-transcendence towards goodness. As knowledgeable people say, this Divine Mother is 'love' as well as 'shakti', 'care' as well as 'rebuke', 'caress' as well as 'smite'. For, the holistic *rishi* view of humankind accepts the reality of an inescapable admixture of the 'good' and the 'bad'. Chapter 16 of the *Bhagwadgita* gives us such a holistic view of man.

The emphasis on 'maternalistic' management may also be justified as a rebuttal of the long-held masculine, left-brained, objectivized Western approach to management. It has, for all these decades, been a lopsided 'paternalistic' ethos. This has been correlated with mounting aggression against Nature and man. Apparently at least, management has thereby emerged more or less as a 'head-full, heart-less' process. For, otherwise how could a human being be called a human resource? Hence, resuscitation of the 'feminine' (not feminist) outlook would be a right effort.

Those who can cast off the thick curtain of fashionable management lore, they should be able to perceive in the author's advocacy of the symbiotic approach of 'masculine-feminine' or '*purusha-prakriti*', the return of holistic ethos. The 'father' alone is adequate. So is the 'mother'. 'Paternalism' is odious. 'Maternalism' too might turn out be so – who knows, (*e.g.*, raging terrorism against the country). Therefore, our word 'parentalism' (not given in the book) is a more authentic fit for the 'heart-cum-head' model espoused in the book.

It is a happy augury that the first list of thirteen values has been derived from sacred literature. Non-humane, even in-human, secularized management will need sustained administration of sacred human values. For instance, greed (non-humane) has become so deep and pervasive, though masked by development or globalization rhetoric, that its containment (at the very least) can only be done by the thorough culture of frugality or contentment. And where else can one find the guidelines for this humanising process but in our sacred heritage. Maternalistic, humanized management will need, at least in the corporate sector, very often to decide whether to maintain fidelity to mother-centric human values if they cause a dent in the bottom line and market valuation. The 3-D framework presented by Rao should help considerably in this task.

This book by Prof. Rao should make a positive impact in neutralizing the fiery masculine tendencies of management in today's hyper-competitive atmosphere. It also offers some useful stock-taking about contemporary work done in the field of human values in India. Therefore, our best wishes to Prof. G.P. Rao and his work.

Aurangabad, Maharashtra **— Prof (Dr.) S.K. Chakraborty**

Founder Convener
Management Centre for Human Values (MCHV)
Indian Institute of Management, Calcutta

Foreword Three

The world need a new vision,
To see the world through a new prism.

'Selfish gene' syndrome has been dominating the thought of the natural scientists as well as social scientists. However, spiritual literature since ancient times has been proposing the idea of 'noble gene' and 'altruistic gene'. It is for the natural scientists to uncover the truth behind such insights. In any case in human society we do find individuals driven by HOPE: Higher Order Purpose of Existence.

In consonance with selfish gene, noble gene and altruistic gene typology and also in consonance with guna dynamics of interplay between tamas, rajas and sattava qualities in human beings, we can formulate, 3Gs model for understanding complexity of human nature in social and organisational contexts. As per this model, 3Gs stand for Greed, Goodness and Godness. While the phrases, Greed and Goodness are widely understood, how should we define, Godness? By Godness we imply realizing the higher purpose of existence. Further it also implies realizing the divinity within. Swami Vivekananda observed that 'every soul is potentially divine, purpose of existence is to realize the divinity'. Godness can also be defined in terms of spiritual qualities of love, compassion and divinity.

In contemporary context, we need to address an important question *viz.*, Should we develop human relationships and thereby human society and its institutions on the basis of Greed, or Goodness combined with Godness? In the corporate context, it implies that Corporations should are not driven by the 'corporate greed', but by higher order purpose of existence such as contribution to society. Corporate leaders like Narayanamurthy talk about 'compassionate capitalism'. However, we need to go a step further in the direction of 'Compassionate and Sustainable Development'. This would be possible, provided we incorporate the dimensions of Goodness and Godness in all human endeavor including economic activities. Western literature related to ethics also emphasizes similar concerns through the ideas of virtue ethics and deontological perspectives.

Prof. G.P. Rao, well known management thinker, researcher and institution builder, with his decades of research in the field of human values has provided us many new insights in his book, Humanising Management: Transformation through Human Values, for developing organisations based on Goodness (dignity) and Godness (divinity). Through '*Spandan*' of his 3 D model of Diagnosis, Discovery and Development with experiential learning consisting of introspection and feedback as its plank, he has shown us a clear path in this direction. This book based on his extensive research is indeed a thought provoking contribution in the field of human values, business ethics and good governance.

Corporate leaders, policy makers, management teachers and management students would find this book extremely useful and inspiring for creating a transformational change through human values in functioning of modern organisations.

Bengaluru, Karnataka

— Prof. (Dr.) Subhas Sharma
Dean, Indian Business Academy,
Bengaluru and Greater Noida.

Prologue

This book on Humanising Management: Transformation through Human Values originates from the belief of the author about human beings. The belief is that all human beings are innately divine. Their innate divinity is manifested through their basic goodness. The basic goodness of human beings is reflected through their desire to be of help to others; to do good without necessarily expecting any return or reward. The innate divinity, basic goodness and the intrinsic altruism of human beings are the crux of human existence. The belief in these three tenets is the driving force for human progress. Human interactions and activities based upon this belief is the touchstone for human harmony. The fountain head of human harmony is the trinity: the three concepts of Mother, *Spandan* and Universal Consciousness. The concept of Mother stands for faith in others and empathy of a high order. *Spandan*, a Sanskrit word, means Heartbeat, Vibration and Pulsation. *Spandan* is symbolic of sensitivity to, and identification with, others. Universal Consciousness represents the ultimate of oneness in all the elements of the universe including human beings. The odyssey of human beings of self diagnosis, discovery and development then reaches its destination: *Satyam* (Truth), *Shivam* (God, the Supreme Power) and *Sundaram* (Beauty). As stated by Jacquelyn Small, the American Spiritual Psychologist, "We are not small human beings trying to be spiritual; we are spiritual beings practicing to be human."

■ Faith in Basic Goodness of Others: A Point of View – A Pointer to Management

Applied to management, the basic goodness is assumed to be in the manager and the managed. The basic goodness, in other words, exists among all the members of the given organisation. The manager tries to do his best and also tries to be helpful to others. The managed try to do their best and also try to be helpful to others. Members of an organisation as a whole thus try to do their best in terms of achieving results and also try to be of help to one another in terms of maintaining harmonious relations. Then why is it that managers, the managed and thus the members of the organsiation as a whole do not always succeed in achieving the results or the relations or both? The answer lies in the fact that so far we have been mentioning about the 'trying' of the managers and the managed. 'Trying' indicates the willingness accompanied by the required effort in achieving the results and maintaining relations. We need however to mention about the nature and extent of willingness and of effort *possessed* by the managers and the managed, as against the *required* willingness and effort in achieving the results and maintaining relations.

Possessed at t_i, t_{ii},.. t_n	Required at t_i, t_{ii}, ..t_n
– Nature of willingness of the managers.	– Nature of willingness of the managers.
– Extent of willingness of the managers.	– Extent of willingness of the managers.
– Nature of efforts of the managers.	– Nature of efforts of the managers.
– Extent of effort of the managers.	– Extent of efforts of the managers.
– Nature of willingness of the managed.	– Nature of willingness of the managed.
– Extent of willingness of the managed.	– Extent of willingness of the managed.
– Nature of efforts of the managed.	– Nature of efforts of the managed.
– Extent of efforts of the managed.	– Extent of efforts of the managed.

The implications about the possible gaps as between and among (*a*) nature and extent; (*b*) managers and the managed; (*c*) possessed and the required; and (d) the different periods of time are far reaching. It is further to be noted that except at the top and at the bottom of the structure of the organisation, every one in an organisation assumes the roles of the manager and the managed. Comprehending these implications and bridging the gaps thus becomes an important task for the management and the organisation.

To comprehend the diversities in human behaviour in work situations and their implications for management, we may understand the simple but the profound truth that behaviour is a function of the self and the situation. Whether an individual could achieve the desired result or not, in other words, depends upon himself and the environment within which he functions. The factors related to self are personality, learning, perception, motivation and attitudes. The environment enveloping an individual consists of family, neighborhood, community, society, country, world and the universe. The behaviour of an individual measured in terms of success or failure is thus the result of interplay of factors related to self and the situation. That this simple and obvious truth is more often than forgotten, that success is attributed to self and that failure is blamed on others is another insight and an issue worthy of introspection and incorporation in the process of one's experiential learning.

When the message of the truth that behaviour is a function of individual and situation is understood, the needed development process becomes clear to the management and the organisation. The first message is 'start with self'. The first step therefore is self diagnosis, self discovery and self development. This is what the crux of *Spandan* approach is: Three D approach of Diagnosis, Discovery and Development with Experiential Learning consisting introspection and feedback as its plank. The process starts with self at individual level, and moves on to the levels of group, organisation and society. This process starts with the faith in the basic goodness of others as credo for manager to humanize management. Faith in basic goodness of others thus becomes core human value in the process.

It is significant to note that the manager in this process of humanising management plays three roles. Since the manager 'targets' himself first for the change process, he becomes the object. Since as part of management as a system of authority, manager decides upon and initiates the change process, he also becomes the subject. Since, finally, it is experiential learning, which is the plank of change and which in essence means 'self learning'/'teaching self, manager becomes verb. The manager thus is the subject, verb and object of the process of humanising management. The knowledge of this insight and its implications for managerial functioning is another input which this book offers to its readers – the functioning and prospective professionals in management.

This is the process of learning with faith in the basic goodness of human beings as credo that the author has had gone through at personal and professional levels spanning around five decades since the early sixties when he got initiated in management as a student. This process, the author believes, is an odyssey, never ending, always nerve breaking but ever enriching. Further, the belief is that this is perhaps the only way for management to transform organisations into 'Functionally Humane' symbolising an optimal balance between Task Function and Social-emotional Function; Results and Relations; and, Head and Heart

To sum up: This is a point of view; and, pointer for management for humanising management. Faith in basic goodness of others is the core human value. Experiential Learning is the plank. The motto is developing Functionally Humane Organisations. The goal is Optimal Balance between Head and Heart in human organisations.

■ Innate Divinity in Human Beings: A Viewing Point – Pointer for Mankind

Beyond management of organisations lies the 'management' of society, nation and the world encompassed by the universe. Innate divinity in human beings is the basic belief and the premise of the book. Innate divinity, as noted, is manifested in the basic goodness of others, and in the desire of human beings to be help to others. The concept of divinity at the level of the universe is known as 'Universal Consciousness'.

This is a viewing point; and pointer to mankind. The motto is remaking ourselves as human beings. The goal is human Harmony.

The odssey of the look, however, ends at making a beginning in this pointer to mankind.

■ Transformation through Human Values

The focus of this book is on management of organisations, i.e: humanising management at individual, group and organisational levels within the framework of the given economy, society and country (Parts II and III of the book). The insights are pointers to the management and constitute the Point of View.

The analysis beyond management of organisations is offered (Part IV) The same set of beliefs about self and others applicable to management at organsiational level are equally applicable at the levels of society, country and the world. These beliefs, as mentioned, are innate divinity, basic goodness and the intrinsic altruism. The insights of the oldest level are pointers to mankind and constitute a Viewing Point.

Transformation through human values is attempted through the concepts of 'mother', '*spandan*' and – culminating in – 'universal consciousness.' 'Mother' stands for, among others, 'faith in goodness of others'. Other equally important characterstics of Mother are: caring, sharing, nurturing and empathy of a high order. The message is that these qualities standing for Mother are to be imbibed and adhered to by manager while dealing with others in work situations. The empathy of high order of Mother is manifested by her ability to understand the need s of her children without being asked. This quality of Mother is symbolized by the concept of '*Spandan*', a Sanskrit word meaning Heartbeat, Vibration and pulsation. The message is that such sensitivity towards others and their needs should be the bedrock of human behaviour not only in work situations but also in all walks of life. Self and Situation lose their boundaries Lower self (pettiness) is replaced by higher Self (dignity and divinity). Self enlarges itself into the Universal Consciousness. This is the Theory of Oneness which recognizes the existence and importance of inner and outer universes. The inseparability of Spirituality and Science is thus reestablished.

This book is a statement of belief that human beings are innately divine and capable of remaking themselves as human beings through self diagnosis, discovery and development. Self thus is the crux of human survival and growth. Self thus signals the beginning of the odyssey from lower self to higher Self.

■ Plan of the Book

The book is divided into four parts.

Part I: The Innate Divinity in Human Beings: Pointers to Management and Mankind

The first part focuses on the cardinal principle of innate divinity being pointer to management and mankind. The first chapter, "The interplay of head and heart in management thinking and action" tries to trace the issue of humanising management, the pointer to management, in terms of the felt need of management to strike an optimal balance between Results and Relations. Chapter two and three develop the theme and postulate that the humanising management, the pointer to management and human harmony, the pointer to mankind, are indeed a continuum. The concepts of mother, *spandan* and universal consciousness are, in other words, linking pins in the process. What an approach emphasisng on self as the key for the transformation process is discussed in chapter four, "*Spandan*: An introduction" The next chapter, chapter five, looks back into the past so as to examine the circumstances which led to the present characterised by skew in favour of a high degree of materialism necessitating 'remaking' of ourselves for future. The last chapter, chapter six, offers an Analytical Framework for this study indicating as to how to go about 'remaking ourselves' at different levels of transformation through human values. The analytical framework is based upon systems thinking and approach.

Part II: *Spandan* Approach and Process

Part II on *Spandan* has three chapters, chapters seven to nine. These deal with the two major methods of transformation, namely Propagation (Chapter 7) and Inculcation (Chapter 8) of human values. The last chapter, Chapter 9, examines the insights and issues emanating from the process of inculcation of human values in management.

Part III: A Point of View: Transformation through Human Values

The human behaviour operates at three planes. These are mental (*manasa*), verbal (*vacha*), and conduct (*karmana*). The components integrating these three planes of human behaviour are Knowledge, Skills and Attitudes. Knowledge refers to awareness, cognition. Skills relate to action, conation. Attitude refers to predisposition of mind, emotions. These three components in other words address the issues of what, how and why of human behaviour respectively.

Human values are considered as strongly held positive attitudes. The relationship between attitude and values and its relevance to the transformation process thus become the focus of the first chapter in this Part (Chapter 10).

The next chapter (Chapter 11) postulates that such transformation gets institutionalized when it becomes part of management philosophy and institution building. Chapters 12 to 14 discuss the transformation of management of self at individual, professional and organisational levels respectively. Instruments developed by the authorities concerned are used as the studies of reference for the analysis. The inputs emanating from these three chapters are compared with the Spectrum of Human Values in Industrial Organisations developed by G. P. Rao. This spectrum of human values is used as the instrument for inculcation of human values in an organisation by *Spandan*. The last chapter, Chapter 16, aims at understanding the role of Community Service as a human value in management philosophy and institution building. Jaipur Rugs Company Pvt. Ltd., Jaipur, India, has been taken as a case study for the purpose.

Part IV: Viewing Point: Beyond Management of Organisations

This part goes beyond the management of organisations. Society and World have been selected as frames of reference. Chapter 17 examines the role of family and education in the orientation of values and their adherence in management and industry. Further, it is argued that the proper role of management in the society is to widen the role of corporate citizenship into that of an organisational citizenship. The next chapter (Chapter 18) focuses on the issues of the management interface with globalization and the mankind's interface with mankind. Globalisation calls for global corporate mindset with corresponding values to be integrated in work ethic and culture. Spiritual democracy recognizes the innate divinity in human beings; and thus becomes a logical corollary of our efforts at conducting ourselves befitting the spiritual dimension of human beings.

The book ends with Epilogue entitled, Back to Self. The Prologue, it may be recalled, underscored the importance of self as the harbinger of self diagnosis, discovery and development. The Epilogue reinforces the same viewpoint by marshalling knowledge and practices from diversified spheres of activity.

Many chapters in the book has Endnotes Containing Notes, Qoutes and References. Select Reflections containing wisdom, insights, experiences and experiments of eminent persons from different walks of life as emanating from the Endnotes are incorporated of the end at the book.

❑❑❑

Acknowledgement

Since long my wife had a desire that a book containing the experiments and experiences of her husband in orientations of values in work life should see the light of the day. Thanks to Mr. Sunil Saxena at Ane Books Pvt. Ltd., New Delhi, Mrs. Rao's desire has been fulfilled. Thanks to the Publishers for an excellent job done.

Contents

Part III: A Point of View: Transformation through Human Values

PART I

The Innate Divinity in Human Beings:

Pointers for Management and Mankind

The first part focuses on the cardinal principle of innate divinity being pointer to management and mankind. The **first chapter**, "The interplay of head and heart in management thinking and action" tries to trace the issue of humanising management, the pointer to management, in terms of the felt need of management to strike an optimal balance between Results and Relations. **Chapter two** and **three** develop the theme and postulate that the humanising management, the pointer to management and human harmony, the pointer to mankind, are indeed a continuum. The concepts of mother, *spandan* and universal consciousness are, in other words, linking pins in the process. What an approach emphasizing on self as the key for the transformation process is discussed in **chapter four**, "*Spandan*: An introduction" The next chapter, **chapter five**, looks back into the past so as to examine the circumstances which led to the present characterised by skew in favour of a high degree of materialism necessitating 'remaking' of ourselves for future. The last chapter, **chapter six**, offers an Analytical Framework for this study indicating as to how to go about 'remaking ourselves' at different levels of transformation through human values. The analytical framework is based upon systems thinking and approach.

1

The Interplay of Head and Heart in Management Thinking and Action

> *The seat of knowledge is in the head, of wisdom in the heart.*
>
> — William Hazlitt

An organisation, while working towards achieving its stated objective(s) as enunciated in its Mission Statement, has essentially to contend with two issues:

1. To complete the given task as effectively as possible; and
2. To complete the task in such a manner that it is the outcome of maximum possible willingness and co-operation on the part of its employees.

The challenge, and therefore opportunity, for management is how to get the given task accomplished well and willingly. Striking an optimal balance between the Task function (Results) and Social emotional function (Relations) thus becomes *sine-qua-non* of effective management.

Substantial management literature and practices on motivation and leadership thus understandably revolves – or should revolve – around this basic issue of evolving, maintaining and improving an optimal balance between results and relations.

Equally understandably, the management thinkers and practitioners could recognize the genesis of this issue in the basic physiological phenomenon of human beings – that of having left and right side of their brain endowed with reason and emotions respectively – the same phenomenon being comprehended as **Head** and **Heart**; Intellect and Intuition, Reason and Emotion; Analytical and Descriptive; Masculine and Feminine; Yin and Yang; West and East.

The Industrial Revolution, spanning nearly hundred years between mid eighteenth and nineteenth centuries heralded the emergence of entirely new economic system characterized by factory organisation, large scale production, huge investments and capitalism. During this phase the emphasis was – perhaps naturally – on production and profits. The subsequent hundred years – till the outbreak of Second World War (1939–1945), to be specific – accelerated the dominance of task function over social emotional function. The consequences are there for all of us to see: work alcoholism, disruption of family system, ugly side of urbanization, social convulsions, economic imbalances, cultural shocks, environmental degradation, etc. Profits, Materialism and Results virtually ejected Service, Spiritualism and Relations, in that order, in the functioning of industrialism. The head, in other words, won over the heart. Human avarice silenced the human conscience.

The celebrated Hawthorne Studies of Elton Mayo and his associates at the General Electric Company, USA (1925–1930) brought out the human and social consequences of factory organisation, mechanization, mass production representing capitalism. More important, however, the Studies led to the emergence of Human Relations Movement in industry. Experiments were conducted to examine the impact of employee participation in matters related to work and shop floor. The results were encouraging. The importance of dignity of labour and the need for treating employees as human beings were emphasized and practised. Creating a sense of belongingness was given priority. Employer employee relations, consequently, improved. The results were not far reaching and enduring. The main reason was that the cordial relations were more because of the interest and involvement of the top man and management- rather than being the effect of the change in the system. Capitalism was, and is, characterized by separation of production from distribution. Capitalist system remaining unchanged, the impact of human relations thus remained rather cosmetic if not superficial. The critique of socialism against human relations was therefore that creation of a mere 'sense' of belongingness while the means of production remained in the hands of capitalists would be counter-productive.

Post Second World War witnessed the formation of United Nations and other related institutions aimed at – among others – countering the *evil* side of industrialization in all its facets. Almost simultaneously, however, scientific and technological developments made quantum jumps leading to Globalisation. In the context of the issue on hand, *viz.*, the interplay of head and heart in management thinking and action, globalisation appears to have two significant and contradictory impacts. Technology demands a high degree of cerebral operation characterized by homogeneity and uniformity to achieve the required competitive edge at industrial and national levels. Cross cultural functioning of management, on the other hand, is characterized by heterogeneity and diversity; and, demands dealing with people of different ethos and traditions in a manner *acceptable* to them, *i.e.*, those managed. Hence, the balancing act between results and relations – head and heart – becomes all the more tricky, indomitable but inevitable.

A Manager is expected to work through and work with others: work through, as a leader with task completion as the focus; and, working with others, as a companion with the required empathy, equation and social emotional wavelength with his team members. Although a few Universities and institutions in our country were offering MBA courses during 50's, India has ushered in professional management education at national level with the creation of Institutes of Management (IIMs) – the first two at Ahmedabad and Calcutta having started their Post Graduate Programme in Management (PGP) during 1964–65. Having been first a student and then a teacher since that period, I observe that management education has had gone through two phases; and, currently going through the third phase, in terms of its enabling prospective professionals develop the required competence in working with and through others. These three phases can be captioned as Communication, Interpersonal Effectiveness and Value Orientation – in that order.

The first phase of emphasis on managerial communication as needed quality continued for the first fifteen to twenty years after the commencement of the postgraduate programme (PGP) in Management by the Indian Institute of Management of Ahmedabad and Calcutta in 1964. Students with public school and convent education background, accordingly, had an edge over others at both the stages of admission in management institutions and of obtaining job offers after completing their studies. Good, flowery and forceful communication enables one to 'reach' the other persons; but does not ensure 'interacting' with others unless the others 'believe' in what is communicated. The emphasis therefore shifted to Interpersonal Effectiveness in mid 80s and lasted for about a decade or so thereafter. A good communicator thus could become effective communicator in the context of his workgroup. For instance, in a three-day workshop on Interpersonal Effectiveness conducted for the Chairman and Managing Director and his 15 immediate senior colleagues of the Mahanagar Telephone Nigam Ltd., (MTNL) in 1998, the participants were requested to identify five elements of interpersonal effectiveness which they thought would enable the MTNL achieve its Mission. The top five responses emerged were as follows: Job knowledge and its sharing 'without ego'; Communication; Receptivity and Sensitivity; Cordial relationship; and Honest approach. This example illustrates as to how the perspective broadened from mere communication to interpersonal relations. Still the effectiveness extended only to the extent of his own department, team and workgroup. In other words, there could be an effective manager, and an effective department – but not necessarily an effective organisation.

Management educators and professionals, accordingly, are currently trying – in yet a small way, however – to grapple with the issues of incorporating human values in management education. The objective is enabling prospective and functioning professionals develop values orientation as an ingredient of their professionalism, and inculcating values as integral to work ethic and culture in the given organisation. It is in this context that the significance of the creation of Management Centre for Human Values (MCHV) at the Indian Institute of Management, Calcutta (IIMC) is to be understood.

Thus, as at the time of the end of nineties when the MCHV was formed at IIM, Calcutta, the situation was as follows:

- **Sixties and Seventies:** Emphasis on managerial communication (at individual level) – PGP at IIMs; MBA courses in Universities and; MDPs by IIMs and others;
- **Eighties:** Emphasis on managerial interpersonal effectiveness (at work group level) – PGP at IIMs; MBA courses in some universities; and MDPs by IIMs and others;
- **Eighties and Onwards:** (*a*) Emphasis on Managerial Values embedded and emanating from Indian ethos: S.K. Chakraborty, Management Centre for Human Values, Indian Institute of Management, Calcutta; and (*b*) Emphasis on Indian values along with soul at altruistic and cosmic levels: Subhash Sharma, Indian Institute of Plantation Management, Bangalore and later Indian Business Academy, Bangalore.
- **Late Nineties and Onwards:** Emphasis on integrating work related Indian values at organisational level with its mission and 'modus operandi'. It is at this point that '*Spandan*' (Heartbeat) as an idea sprouts and assumes the shape of an instrument in the form of '*Spandan*', an NGO, for translating this idea into a reality, through its 3-D Process.

The genesis and evolution of the concepts of 'Mother' (empathy of highest order) and ,'*Spandan*' (Heartbeat, Vibration) has had gone through two broad phases. The first phase relates to their application to the management at individual, professional and organisational levels. The second phase relates to their application at the levels of society, world and the universe. During the first phase, the concept of management is used as manager and management in their professional terms. During the second phase, the concept of management is used in its generic sense – free from its professional identity. During the first phase, we talk in terms of management 'of' organisation; and, during the second phase, we talk in terms of management 'and' society and universe at large.

In terms of progression of thinking, the first phase represents 'Point of View'; and the second 'Viewing Point'. The primary objective of this book is to offer a process of inculcation of values as instrumental for achieving balance between **Results** and **Relations** (Point of View) in an organisation. This process and approach emanates from the experiential learning and participant observation of the writer as a student of human behavior for the last forty years or so.

Going beyond the spheres of organisation, industry and economy, the interplay of Head and Heart at international level specific to globalization can – and needs to – be evolved towards optimal balance between Economic Growth and Social Justice, symbolizing human growth and human justice as a whole. Not surprisingly, Globality calling for – and as a means of – correcting the 'flip side', so to say, of Globalisation is assuming greater importance. The concept of '*Spandan*' (Heartbeat, Vibration) becomes equally relevant for coping with these issues effectively.

The issues of the Point of view and Viewing points beckoning management and mankind are discussed further in the next two chapters.

❑❑❑

2

Humanising Management: A Point of View and A Viewing Point

> *Being willing to change allows you to move from a point of view to viewing point – a higher, more expansive place, from which you can see both sides.*
>
> — Thomas Crum

2.1 A Point of View and A Viewing Point

The issue on hand is one of growth, development and transformation. The transformation is by management, of management and for management. The odyssey of transformation is initiated by management primarily within the framework of the given organisation. The transformation is of managers and management at individual, professional, organisational and societal levels. The transformation aims at propagating and inculcating required knowledge, skills, attitudes and values for enabling managers and management become 'functionally humane'. The managers and management thus become subject, predicate and object of the process of self transformation. The pivot of growth, development and transformation is thus self-elevation of lower self of pettiness to higher Self of divinity.

The above is a **Point of View**, and, a **Pointer for the Management**. The expected end result being optimal balance between Results and Relations in an organisation leading to its transformation into a Functionally Humane Organisation.

Managers and Management are a segment of human beings. Similarly, management occurs whenever there is need for getting things done through and with others. In a generic sense, therefore, transformation of human beings, like that of managers, is by human beings, of human beings and for human beings. Managerial transformation and transformation of human beings thus become co-extensive. For human beings the motto is to move from lower self (pettiness) to higher Self (dignity) (S.K. Chakraborty). "To remake ourselves", as Mahatma Gandhi, would have said: "As human beings our greatness lies not so much in remake the world – which is the myth of atomic age – as in being able to remake ourselves."

The above is a **Viewing Point** and hence a **Pointer for Mankind**. The expected end result is Human Harmony.

We therefore move from a point of view to a viewing point. Thomas Crum once said: "Being willing to change allows you to move from a point of view to a viewing point – a higher, more expansive place, from which you can see both sides." This is the essence of growth, development and transformation of managers, management and of mankind as a whole.

2.2 The Viewing Point: The Innate Divinity in Human Beings

The origin of Universe, of mankind and of the nature of human beings, are among the issues which have been fascinating thinkers, scientists alike since time immemorial.

The answers to these issues are still however evasive and uncertain. Big Bang theory estimates the origin of universe of billions of years and of mankind a few million years. Most widely accepted view of anthropological studies on the subject places the first appearance of human beings at two million years ago.

Similarly, about the basic human nature, the views are mixed. Based upon fossils discovered in South Africa, biological theories viewed till 1970s' human beings as archetypal aggressors "blood-be smattered archives of history". Eric Fromm, for example, in his classic, "The Anatomy of Human Destructiveness", observed: "Man is the only mammal who is a large scale killer and a sadist." Discoveries in the 1970s' however have tended to emphasize the Cooperative Man. Anthropological studies on the subject tend to endorse this point of view. Among human hunter-gatherers, the anthropologists maintain, the sharing of meat is law – a means of insisting that "we are one."

All religions, faiths and ethical canons emphasize the basic goodness and inherent divinity in human beings. In Islam, for instance, Sufi thought is centered around the two fundamental doctrines of the Transcendent Unity of Being or *wahdut al-wujud* and the universal or perfect man, *al-insan al-kamil*. The concept of fana or annihilation of ego is at the very heart of Sufi philosophy. It is therefore not surprising that a Sufi proverb goes to the extent of saying, "I searched for

God and found only myself. I searched for myself and found only God." Similarly, in Srimad Bhagavaatm 11.4, it is stated: 'Thou seest reality in the transitory body because of ignorance. Remove this ignorance that veils the true knowledge, and know thy self as pure, free, divine, absolute.'

■ Rekindling the Innate Divinity

- □ Why it is that such divinity is not manifested in human behaviour?
- □ Why is it that evil overshadows virtue?
- □ Why is it that misery and unhappiness has become a rule and joy and happiness an exception in human life?

According to **Dalai Lama**, *"The world at large is entangled in problems which are human created"*.

Since the problems are 'human created', the solution should also come from humans. As **S. Radhakrishnan**, the eminent philosopher and the former President of India stated, *"The man creates problems and solves them"*.

The human being has also the innate capacity to think of solutions to the problems created by himself. **Grace Light** and **Hidden Energy** are the two relevant cues in this context:

> **Grace Light:** It symbolizes the light of God or powerful cosmic energy which has power to change our lives. In Tamil, Grace Light is called *Arul.* Arul is defined as soul intelligence, as opposed to *marul* which means of mind intelligence… Grace light will bring a new type of consciousness beyond logic with flowering of the heart centre.
>
> **Hidden Energy:** Swami Vivekananda poses, in his typical way, the question: Do you know how much energy, how many powers, how many forces are still lurking behind that frame of yours? What scientist has known all that is in man? Vivekananda then answers: Millions of years have passed since man first came here and yet but one infinitesimal part of his powers has been manifested.

Equally important, is that the human being has responsibility to think of the solutions. The only and real issue is whether he comes to know of his responsibility; and if he does when and how. The realisation may not take place. It may take long time. Or, just an observation or an emotion may trigger the realisation. Two classic examples of such a change of heart are hunter turned saint Valmiki, the author of the epic Ramayana and emperor Ashoka, the king turned propagator of Buddhism, a religion of love and compassion. It was the sight of the veiling of the bird on its companion bird being killed by him, the hunter, which changed the heart of Valmiki. Similarly, it was the sight of agony and cries of the women and children whose kith and kin were massacred by his armies in Kalinga that brought a wave of repentance in Ashoka.

■ The Innate Divinity, Functionally Humane Organisation and Human Harmony

The author has had opportunities in understanding the human behaviour for over four decades. These opportunities arose in his roles as a teacher, researcher, trainer, consultant and institution builder in management – and, finally, since 2001, as Founder Chairman of *Spandan*, a voluntary organisation committed to propagation and inculcation of human values in management and society. Further, since he had been a student of management in the first batch of a national institute of management (IIM, Calcutta), 1964–67, and continued being a teacher since then, his career in management education, and, the growth of management education and its interface with industry in the country got intertwined and became coextensive. This work thus becomes in a way an autobiographical introspect of the author.

Based upon the experiences and insights gained through these opportunities, the author comes to rather an unusual – one may, as well say, 'quixotic' – insight about understanding and working with and through others. Working with others denotes working with persons placed at same or similar levels as one's own who is interacting (Focal Person). These include colleagues, peers, friends, associates etc. These are human interactions at lateral level. Working through others denotes working with persons whose performance becomes the responsibility of one's own or those who are placed at lower than one's own who is interacting (Focal Person). These are human interactions at vertical level.

The insight is that understanding and working with and through others is at once most difficult and most easy. Most difficult, till one fails to develop equation with others based upon mutual love, trust and respect. The equation with others could be functional, professional and personal. The others to be interacted within the given organisation include immediate superiors, colleagues and peers, and, subordinates. Once the equation comprising essentially mutual love, trust and respect is created, developed and maintained, working with and through others becomes most easy. The entire and only challenge facing all concerned in management education and profession thus is just this: How to create, develop and maintain such an equation, wavelength, chemistry, bond and vibration as integral to work ethic and culture at organisational level so that a Funtionally Humane Organisation is created. (Point of view).

Going beyond management of organisations, similar challenge of developing the equation faces human beings at the levels of society, country, world and the universe. (Viewing point)

Significantly, the answer to the challenges of developing equation at the level of organisations for management and at the other levels for the mankind in general lies in one particular insight. The insight at conceptual level is the **knowledge** (Awareness) and **belief** (Acceptance) in the innate divinity in human beings. The innate divinity manifests itself as basic goodness in the emotional component of human personality.

The basic goodness results in predisposition and inclination of human beings to be helpful to others as an attitude. This attitude of being helpful ('Awareness'), over a period time, due to belief (Acceptance) and adherence (Action), becomes the orientation of values or mindset ('*manasa*'). Such mindset ('*manasa*'), I believe, consists of three fundamental and universal values: **Love and compassion, Trust and Respect**. These three values translate themselves suitably in the sayings and doings ('*vacha*' – communication and '*karmanya*' – action) of the human beings concerned.

- **Love and compassion** manifests itself in (*a*) Creating; (*b*) Nurturing; (*c*) Caring and sharing; and (*d*) Sacrifice.
- The behavioural manifestation of **Trust** is threefold: (*a*) Believing; (*b*) Relying; and (*c*) Delegating.
- **Respect** is manifested in (*a*) "not dehumanising even the enemy" (Mahatma Gandhi); and (*b*) Trying to understand and support the others' viewpoints, even if these viewpoints differ from their own; and (*c*) Upholding the dignity of others.

The end result of the innate divinity in human beings passing through the phases of human personality, attitudes, values and the resultant human behaviour is Human Harmony.

2.3 Point of View: Basic Goodness in Human Beings

When applied to a manager as a focal person, the foregoing insights and analysis underlines the following:

- The importance of manager; having faith in the basic goodness of others as his credo ('*manasa*', mindset); which should be reflected in his sayings ('*vacha*', communication) and doings ('*karmanya*', behaviour); in terms of his adherence to the values of Love and compassion, Trust and Respect; so that others perceive in his interactions with them the reflection of the said values; and are motivated to reciprocate in their own performance; thus paving the way for human values becoming integral to work ethic and culture; and (g) developing and organisation with an optimal balance between Results (Functional) and Relations (Humane); and which can be called as Functionally Humane Organisation.

2.4 Faith in the Basic Goodness of Others as Management Assumption

A teacher of us in management started his first session with the class with the sentence that Behaviour is a function of Individual and Situation.

$$B = f\,i\,,\,s$$

This equation is so simple and innocent in its appearance, but so deep and insightful in its ramifications to human behaviour.

When applied to manager as a focal person, the equation would mean that his behaviour, performance and effectiveness are all the result of him as an **Individual** and the environment within which he is functioning as his **Situation** (context.) Factors related to manager as an individual include his personality, learning, perception, motivation, attitudes and values. Factors related to his environment include his family, friends, peer groups, community, profession and its ethics, and his country and its culture.

An important concept which is generic to manager as an individual and critical to understanding his behaviour and philosophical moorings as a manager is his 'Assumption about others'. Assumptions about others relate to the image, picture, opinion and perceptual map a manager has about others as a whole. One way of looking at the issue is as to what he thinks of others in terms of their goodness, and their willingness to be of help to others. Managerial assumptions about others' goodness can, I submit, be broadly of five categories or levels:

1. That others are **wholly good;**
2. That others are **basically good;**
3. That whether others are **good or bad, I do not know;**
4. That others are **basically bad;** and,
5. That others are **wholly bad.**

Which of these five assumptions is practised most again depends upon the individual and situational factors referred to. What is important is to identify which of these is more desirable, practicable and therefore preferable over the other assumptions.

The first and the last assumptions are that others are wholly good (No. 1); and, that others are wholly bad (No. 5). These two assumptions are not realistic because they ascribe the entire influence either to the individual or to the environment. This is not plausible because thereby these assumptions are also negating the influence whatsoever to the other factor respectively.

The remaining three assumptions are that others are basically good (No.2), that 'I do not know' (No.3) and that others are basically bad (No.4). These assumptions are realistic and plausible. However, the fourth assumption is negative in its connotation, where as the third is neutral. Accordingly these two, (*i.e.*, No.3 and No.4) assumptions would have their own influence on the interplay of head and heart with reference to self image, leadership and motivation. While, therefore, they are realistic and plausible, these assumptions are not desirable – particularly when compared to the remaining assumption, *viz.*, that others are basically good.

The assumption that others are basically good (No.2) thus stands as realistic, plausible and desirable compared to the other four assumptions. Further this assumption is congruent with the normative approach of the present study.

To sum up

1. That others are wholly good – **Not realistic, not plausible.**
2. That others are basically good – **Realistic, plausible, positive.**
3. That whether others are good or bad, I do not know – **Realistic, plausible but neutral.**
4. That others are basically bad – **Realistic, plausible but negative.**
5. That others are wholly bad – **Not realistic, not plausible.**

■ Faith in Basic Goodness as Management Assumption

Keeping the normative frame of mind of management in view, however, it is clear that the second assumption that others are basically good deserves further scrutiny. Accordingly relevant illustrations, reflections and institutions are mentioned below:

- Asked, 'What is the largest thing in the smallest container?', Periander, the Greek Philosopher (600 BC), replied: "Good sense in a human brain."
- Peter F. Drucker , the celebrated management thinker, stated in his seminal work, "The Practice of Management", "the human being is the central, rarest, most precious capital resource of our society".
- J.R.D. Tata: "There is a belief in our country that our culture and our character cannot allow our people to attain consistently high standards;

that shoddiness and carelessness are our God – given ways of life. But if faith in them, you ask our men for their best, they rise to a belief in their work and create momentum towards improvement. Often I have seen men who were considered ordinary, rise to extraordinary heights."

- Club of Rome, the informal organisation founded in 1968 by a small group of individuals from 10 countries, is another example of human being held in esteem. Dedicated to an understanding of the global system, Club of Rome believes that "man is not only a biological organism, or an economic unit, but in all his manifestations. Man is a spiritual and rational creature, a playful one, an artistic and dreaming one; we consider him in the work span of his personality and not just as a body and a customer."
- Walter Pucky, a British industrialist and a self-made man, wrote a book with autobiographical touch. In the preface to the book, Walter Pucky (1967) recorded, "Top managers could rise top status only if they recognized, and genuinely acted upon the belief , that every person in the group wanted to help and would work better if he knew better how he could help."
- Ajit N. Haksar spent his entire career in ITC Ltd. and reached the top as Chairman of the Company. While addressing his last Annual General Meeting as Chairman of the Company in 1984, Ajit Haksar, narrated his growth in the Company, the troubles and tribulations he and his family had to undergo in the process. He however states at the end that what he remembers and cherishes is that "I believe that people, in any status of life, will ever respond to warmth and friendship".

One thus appears to be on the right track of humanising the management and mankind with innate divinity in human beings as the credo. The next chapter aims at understanding as to how we move from the point of view to the viewing point.

Endnotes

Human Beings: Their Potential

1. **S. Radhakrishnan,** Indian Philosopher and former President of India: There is so much of inequality, so much of injustice in this world. It is the human individual who has to realize that God is the spark in him.

2. **Reinhold Neibuhr,** American Theologist: Man's capacity for justice makes democracy possible, but man's inclination to injustice make democracy necessary.

3. **Peter Drucker,** American Management Thinker: The human being is the central, rarest most precious capital resource of our society.

4. **Sufi Proverb:** I searched for God and find only myself. I searched for myself and find only God'.

5. **Carl Jung,** Swiss Psychological Thinker: As far as we can discern, the sole purpose of human existence is to kindle a light in the darkness of mere being.

6. **The Upnishad:** The little space within the heart is as great as the last universe. The heavens and the earth are there and the sun and the moon and the stars. Fire and the lightening and wings are there and all that now is and all that is not.

7. **Jacquelyn Small,** American Spiritual Psychologist: We are not small human beings trying to be spiritual; we are spiritual beings practicing to be human.

Human Beings: Their Flipside

1. **Mother Teresa:** Violence is within us.

2. **Aldous Huxley,** British Writer: Pleasure cannot be shared; like pain, it can only be experienced or inflicted, and when we give pleasure to our lovers or bestow charity upon the needy, we do so, not to gratify the object of our Benevolence, but only ourselves.

3. **Isaac B. Singer,** Polish Nobel Laureate, for Literature: Man is a caricature of God, a parody of the spirit, the only entity in creation which could be a lie.

4. **Salman Rushdie,** a British Indian Novelist: But human beings do not perceive things whole: we are not Gods but wounded creatures, cracked lenses, capable only of fractured perceptions. Partial beings, in all the senses of that phrase. Meaning is a shaky edifice we build out of scraps, dogmas, childhood injuries, news paper articles, chance remarks, old films, small victories, people hated, and people loved; perhaps it is because our sense of what is the case is constructed from such inadequate materials that we defend it so fiercely, even to the death.

5. **Henri Nouwen,** Dutch Catholic Priest and Writer: Much violence is based on the illusion that life is a property to be defended and not to be shared.

6. **Don Marquis,** American Author: The chief obstacle to the progress of the human race is the human race.

7. **The Buddha:** It is wrong to think that misfortunes come from the East or from the West. They originate within from one's own mind. Therefore it is foolish to guard against misfortunes from the external world and leave the inner mind uncontrolled.

8. **The Dalai Lama:** The problems we face today are human created.

9. **Erich Fromm,** German Social Psychologist: Man is the only mammal who is a large scale killer and a sadist.

10. **Woody Allen,** American Filmmaker: The only thing standing between me and greatness is me.

11. **Fredrick Nietzsche,** German Philosopher: Whenever I climb, I am followed by a dog called ego.

12. **Swami Vivekananda:** No individual is perfect; we are more or less imperfect.

13. **G.G.N. Byron, The British Thinker:** What an antithetical mind ! –tenderness, roughness; delicacy, coarseness, sentiment sensnating; soaring and glovelling; dirt and dirty–all mixed up is that one compound of inspired clay.

❑❑❑

3

Moving from Point of View to Viewing Point: Mother, Management, *Spandan* and Human Harmony

> *Successful companies are whole, wholistic, holy, spiritual companies. All of the excellent companies have an overriding concern for the whole person, the employees, the suppliers, the customers and other stakeholders.*
>
> — Thomas Peters and Robert Waterman
>
> *... but the most wonderful of all (I have seen) is to find that beneath all these apparent variations of manners and customs of culture and power, beats the same mighty human heart under the impulsion of the same joys and sorrows, of the same weakness and strength.*
>
> — Swami Vivekananda

3.1 The Mother, *Spandan* and Management of Organisations: The Point of View

My first 'brush', so to say, with the relevance of the concept of Mother in management came to me when I was a student of management during early '60s. G. Ramanujam, the then trade union leader, who subsequently rose to become Governor of Goa, compared workers with baby sitters. Just as a baby sitter who is paid for looking after the child for a specific period during the absence of the mother, can not consider herself as mother of the child, a worker in a factory cannot consider himself as a 'mother' of the factory. The trade union leader was discussing the problem of employee identification with the organisation in a system of capitalism and free enterprise where capital and labour are separated.

The second occasion of my understanding of the role of mother in management came to me as a researcher. I was studying, during mid '70s, Industrial Relations in a large nationalized bank which has had been honoured with the Best Industrial Relations Award, 1975 by the Federation of Indian Chambers of Commerce and Industry (FICCI). I was interviewing a lady member of a staff of the bank, and was asking her the rather standardized questions: Whether she would leave the Bank if she was offered less than what she was getting in the bank; – if she was offered the same as what she was getting; and, – if she was offered more than what she was getting in the bank. To all the three questions, her answer was 'No'. I further asked her as to why she would not leave even when she was offered more than what she was earning in the bank. Her spontaneous answer was: 'Bank is my mother. Can I leave my mother?' This experience also relates to the issue of employee identification with the organisation, but brings out the typical Indian attitude of referring to any respectable and loved entity as Mother.

The other implication is that it is possible to 'see', 'perceive' and 'identify' mother in other than own biological mother – and accordingly, sense of respect and reverence. It therefore means that if the management and leadership can generate that sense of respect and identification among its employees towards their organisation, then the outcome would be an optimal balance between its Results and relations.

This leads me to my next, third, experience in enhancing my understanding of the relevance of the concept of Mother to management. Such an experience in enriching my understanding on the role of Mother had literally 'happened' in 1981. I had been asked by a College to talk to its faculty and students of management as to 'Which style of Management would suit India?' At that time I was in Madurai Kamaraj University, Madurai; and, was travelling by bus from Madurai to Thiruchendur, an overnight journey of about four hours. I was while travelling asking myself as to which of the four key styles of management would be appropriate for India: Authoritarian; Paternalistic; Constitutional (Legalistic); or, Democratic Participative? In a country of the size of a subcontinent such as India, all the four styles could be found being practised – from highly successful to highly unsuccessful. Each style would be functional in a given set of circumstances; and, no style would be functional under all circumstances. All of a sudden a boisterous noise broke my chain of thoughts. The noise came from an infant from the lap of her mother shouting boisterously and uncontrollably. The father tried to control the child by shouting at her and asking her to shut up. The child, in turn, continued shouting more uncontrollably –

and later, by crying. Then the mother quietly took a poopsie and put it in the mouth of the child. The child instantly became calm and concentrated her attention on enjoying poopsie This came as a sudden and significant realization in my life: Maternalistic Management .Failure of external control as symbolized by father figure; and, success of understanding the needs of others and acting accordingly as characterised by Mother. Here was the child with energy and enthusiasm not knowing how to use. Father trying by controlling; and mother by understanding the need of the child – that of unspent energy – and being successful in channelising the energy when she put poopsie in the mouth of the infant. Maternalistic Management thus came as an answer to the question. A style inspired by the concept of Mother and characterized by certain relevant qualities like empathy, a high degree of sensitivity, nurturing, self-sacrifice and compassion , would thus be – I submit – most suitable for Indian conditions. King Janaka, the father of Sita, in the epic of Ramayana, for example, is known to have identified himself as the mother of his subjects.

The touchstone of such a quality of leading by empathy of high order resulting in identification of self with all other human beings, living organisms and inanimate objects, I believe, emanates from one's willingness and ability to understand the others' needs without being asked. Although deep asleep, the alertness with which a mother comforts her child the moment the child moves a little is a classic example of the sensitivity of the mother towards her child. I submit that this is the quality which any person assigned the responsibility of leading others is required to acquire and reflect in his behavior to be a leader in its true sense. The Sanskrit word *Spandan* tries to capture the spirit of such a quality sought in a leader. Heartbeat, vibration, resonance and echo are some words from English which are nearer to the concept of *Spandan*.

Perusal of literature and management practices world over, however, indicates that the maternalstic style is also a universal phenomenon. For instance, Moe Grzelakowski, the top female executive in the international high tech industry, who broke the glass ceiling at AT&T's Bell Laboratories, Motorola and Dell, weaves together the common leadership threads of 50 remarkable executives and outlines the 'maternal leadership' model. Leading through empathy is considered as a particularly female quality among them.

Very similar to this way of thinking relates to the Masculinity-Femininity dimension of the celebrated Four Dimensional Model of Management Styles of Geert Hofstede. Hofstede provides an insight into national cultural side as it related to hardness/assertiveness and softness and nurturance of the given country.

Masculinity-Femininity thinking emanates from an earlier understanding of human being in terms of left and right sides of human brain. The left side represents intellect, reasoning, logic, quantity and Yin. The right side of the human brain represents intuition, imagination, emotions, quality and Yang.

The Mother's Ministry of Management as being practised since long as credo in Aurobindo Ashram at Pondicherry (India), (1990) stands as a living example and standing monument for Mother's qualities becoming integral with work ethic and a way of life. Certain characteristics of the Mother's Ministry of Management are as follows:

- **Prerequisites of Her Management Philosophy:** Faith and sincerity.
- **Approach:** Consciousness
- **Tool:** Harmony in thoughts and actions within and with others.
- **Aim:** Perfection.

A high degree of sensitivity and a sense of oneness with even inanimate objects like stones and the belief that they are equally prone to pleasure and pain through human touch and treatment is symbolic of maternal character of empathizing and identification with all in the environment.

3.2 *Spandan*, Mother Goddess and The Divine Essence of the Universe: A Viewing Point

Further understanding of the concept of *Spandan* (Heartbeat and Echo) in its historic perspective I believe offers new insights in the functioning of management, human relationships and of human interface with environment. The Tukamo tribe of the Columbian rain forest define the human being as "one who sees and hears the echo and thus knows". This echo or Kesori is the essence of things and 'hearing with echo' refers to knowing what it is that is being perceived, what it is that is being symbolized; not all people can hear it all the time. (G. Geichel-Dolmatoff, an anthropologist – quoted by Marquerite Theophil, in The Fabric of Creation Essence and its echo, The Times of India, August 11, 2000).

An early reference to the concept – its equivalent, to be more appropriate- of *Spandan*, *i.e.*, communicating/receiving communication without any visible means of communication, relates to Jain Sutra Mahavira, the originator of Jainism was silent for years. He did not express any Sutra by speech or by writing. But his 11 disciples continued to be by his side all through. They observed and felt Mahavira's silent vibrations. Whatever each one of them heard within himself, separately, was all alike. What the 11 disciples heard was identical. They wrote down the same. And that is called Jain Sutra. (Amrita Pritam, "Fifty Fragments of Inner self.")

Yoga Vasishta (Sage Vasishta's precepts to Sri Rama) states: "Vibration and consciousness are inseparably like the whiteness of snow, the oil in the sesame seed, the fragrance of the flower and the heat of fire." Based upon this understanding, Sri Aurobindo the great Indian thinker, develops the concept of Power of Mastery. "...mastery means the knowledge of handling certain vibrations; if you know how to handle these vibrations you have the mastery." Extending the logic, so to say, Gary Sobers, a researcher of the Aurobindo Ashram, Aurovillo, Pondicherry, India, first came out in mid 70's with a doctoral thesis on Consciousness Approach of Management postulating that it was possible to influence the behaviour of other from afar. He then demonstrated the same in Chrysler plant in US.

Rhonda Byrne, in her recent work, "Secret" (2006), reveals that 'the most powerful law in the Universe' which she says is based upon the common teaching behind the world's most powerful philosophies and religions. The book posits that human beings have the power to turn up any suffering or weakness into strength, a power, a successful story with just the help of our thoughts and feelings. This is because of what Byrne calls "the power of attraction", of "like attracts like".

No wonder, Helen Keller states that "the best and most beautiful things in the world cannot be seen, nor touched... but are felt in the heart."

My horizon of understanding of human behaviour during this, fourth, phase has, as can be noted, broadend from management of organisations to the management of the world and the universe. The logic and essence remained the same, *viz.*, the innate divinity in the human beings and the universe. The difference is that at the levels of individual, group, institutional and societal levels, the emphasis is on the basic goodness of human beings- its awareness, acceptance and adherence. At the levels of the world and its interface with the universe, the consciousness of innate divinity of human beings expands, transcends and envelops the universe in the form of Universal Consciousness and the 'divine essence of the universe'. (S.M. Bhasker, 2009).

Similarly, the driving force, the Mother, as a symbol remains the same. The difference however is that the divinity and highest degree of sensitivity and empathy of the mother were applied in managing people at individual, group, institutional and societal levels. At global and universal levels, the Mother assumes the role of Earth, the compassionate Mother Goddess (S.M. Bhasker 2009), and as Shakti, the divine mother (Deepak Chopra, 2008).

S.M. Bhasker, in his thoughtful write up, The Environmental Crisis Has A Bright Side, Too, (Times of India, February 16, 2009) states: "In Indic tradition, the earth is worshipped as the compassionate Mother Goddess. It is believed that in her maternal aspect humankind not only find material needs or transcendental aspirations fulfilled but a chance to realize total Reality, God or Supreme Consciousness. This belief may have had a scientific basis, now obscured."

On Shakti being the divine mother, Deepak Chopra (2008) observes: "The all pervading energy source of existence, or Shakti manifests itself as creation. Shakti is the divine mother who gives birth to and nurtures the new born – whether it is a newborn baby, a brand new relationship, afresh idea, or a magical manifestation. Although Shakti is beyond the boundaries of gender, form or colour, we call it Mother because of its mothering and creative qualities."

A recent addition in this line of thinking relates to the work, "The Cosmic Detective – Exploring the Mysteries of our Universe" (2008). The book postulates that while science has helped to get rid of superstition to some extent, we need to continue asking the question as to why we are here." The author of the book, Mani Bhaumik, a Physicist, stated in an interview: "I do think there is a higher power. While we are more used to the power of being an abstract one as the Vedic Brahman, the Western notion of that power is in God as a person. To the skeptics, God is a stranger. But there is no such thing as a stranger; only friends you have not yet met.... As a physicist in quest of knowledge, both the outer and inner universes are important to me. Many physicists are now talking like Vedic philosophers."

When understood, interpreted and attempted in this fundamental sense of being the cosmic force of ***Spandan*** **('heartbeat')**, the concept of Mother and its accompanying empathy and sensitivity of highest order becomes a metaphor, message and means for humanising work and the world order. The mankind in such a situation would be on the path of what Swami Vivekananda had stated as Spiritual Democracy. Speaking at the celebrated World Parliament of Religions in Chicago in 1893, Swami Vivekananda defines Spiritual Democracy based upon Vedantic Philosophy as "the recognition of divinity in every man and woman" and "everybody's inherent right to liberation or "moksha".

❑❑❑

4

Spandan: An Introduction

> *(In Indian context) in the ethics, the first rule of right conduct starts from the urge of the mother, to identify herself with her child in pain or pleasure and seek the common good. It proceeds in ever widening circles of such identification till it includes the whole of humanity.*
>
> — **V. Subramanya Iyer**
>
> *Management works in the system. Leadership works on the system.*
>
> — **Stephen R. Covey**

Spandan as an NGO originated over a period of time as a result of the academic and research interest of the author complemented by the felt need of the nineteen organisations involved in the study on Human Values in Industrial Organisations (G.P. Rao, 1996). The study started as an investigation on relative importance of self control as a human value in work situation. In the course of interviewing with the heads of these organisations, the respondents suggested that the process of implementing the 3-D approach could as well be initiated in their organisations as part of the research work.

The research work thus transformed itself into a collaborative effort by the author and the participating organisations in integrating values with their work culture. By its very nature, therefore, the ***Spandan*** 3-D process was not a document offered by a consultant but a process of working together through trial and error methods and never ending self corrections and improvements. This is a weakness as well as the strength of this process.

We now try to recapture the occasions, experiences and experiments marking certain turning points in the evolution of the ***Spandan Approach*** and the Process.

4.1 The Concept of Mother and Maternalistic Management

The concept of Mother, developed as Maternalistic Management, was published in 1981. The article attracted attention from all walks of life and was greeted with, as the saying goes, both 'Bouquets and Brickbats'. The concept of mother symbolizing the sensitivity of the mother in understanding the needs of the child without being asked was accepted and appreciated as a powerful message and motivator.

Swami Yuktananda of Vivekananda Nidhi, Calcutta, in a letter to the author, wrote:

> "I deeply appreciate the deep psychological insight of mother concept and its multi faceted relatedness not only to work situations but also to work life.
>
> I have gone through some of the puja rituals and can see that the whole approach is psychosomatic in quality improvement on the basis of holism – concept and at that almost an organic view. If you and your team will go deeper into the psychological aspect of Patanjala's Yogadarshan, Bhagavat Gita and the common search for the identity of the self (individual), you will find assured methods to develop managerial attitudes by suing the imaginations and images, faith and belief to the advantage. Just an illustration: Visada (depression) has been transformed into yogo in the very first chapter of Gita".

The critique of the concept of Mother, on the other hand, was two fold. The first was that the concept was outdated and irrelevant; to the extent of being, as was pointed out by a senior administrator, "A grand mother's recipe." The other criticism was that although desirable, it is not practicable to implement in a corporate environment. Students of management schools, for example, used to raise this issues of the approach being difficult to be implemented. When something is found useful, but felt difficult to implement, the way out is not to give up but to do one's best to translate the desirable into reality.

■ The Values Relevant for Management

The next issue relates to the values relevant to the concept of Mother and the application of the values to Maternalistic Management. Thirteen values were identified as organically related to the concept of mother. These values originated from:

(a) Religion and Revelations

(b) Scriptures and Epics; and

(c) Deliberations with the industrial organisations and other institutions.

These 13 values were:

1. Self-identification with others
2. Seeking common good
3. Scrupulous avoidance of injury to others
4. Self-restraint
5. Self-sacrifice in life
6. Patience and tolerance
7. Experiencing the joy of creation
8. Compassion
9. Moral Courage
10. Empathy of the highest order
11. Trust
12. Forgiving nature and
13. Possessiveness

Of the above 13 values, four values were considered suitable enough to be adhered in industrial organsiations. These were:

1. Self-identification with others (Role identification)
2. Patience and tolerance
3. Empathy of the highest order
4. Trust

Another value, Humane approach, was added covering certain other values of the concept, included in the list of thirteen values like Scruplous avoidance of injury to others; Patience and Tolerance; and, Compassion.

The above five values as finally emanated from the concepts of Mother and Maternalistic Management form integral part of the Spectrum of Values of the Work Situations developed by the author.

David Kimber, a fellow academician from Australia, while agreeing to the to the relevance of the concept felt that feminine values and practicability of them in work situations might be difficult, because "could it be that modern bureaucracies impose 'roles' on individuals which are seen to be incompatible with spiritual values?".

Kimber is correct. It is however gratifying to note that corporate culture is slowly but surely realising the relevance of spiritual approach in the management and work culture. As Shri Shri Ravi Sankar, the founder of Art of living succinctly observed spirituality has moved from Pooja Rooms to Board Rooms (Times of India, Guest Editor, Dec. 31, 2008).

4.2 Human Values in Industrial Organisations

The first study in the field of Human Values in industrial orgnisations was undertaken by the author as Sir Ratan Tata Visiting Fellowship (1995–96) which was offered by the Management Centre for Human Values (MCHV) of IIM Calcutta. The study was entitled "Human Values in Industrial Organisations: Feminine Perspective" (Rao, G.P. 1996). The women respondents from academia, management profession, administration and student community were taken as respondents. The objective was to understand the perception of the respondents in terms of the desirability and practicability of personal values and of organisational values in there career. A set of twenty one value dyad was developed on which the respondents were to assess.396 respondents, out of whom 22 were from abroad, representing a cross section from India and abroad participated in the study as respondents.

The study offered certain vistas which were at once insightful and disturbing; insightful because of the very subtle shades in human thinking; and, disturbing because of the nature of such vistas revealing the unwillingness and by or inability of human beings in doing something which they themselves considered as desirable. One such vista relates to the finding on value dyad of Self Control – Controlling Others. Self Control was perceived by the respondents as the second most desirable value (out of 42 values) in an industrial organisation The same respondents however, perceived that it was controlling others that was practised most in industrial organisations.

It so happened that an opportunity did arise to continue the lead for further investigation in the form of second research study as Emeritus Fellowship (1999-2002) offered by All India Council for Technical education (AICTE). The study entitled "Self Control as a Managerial Value" (Rao, G.P. 2002, Mimeo), started as a typical research work, consisting administering response sheet and conducting in depth interview. The respondents of the study comprising 285 top and senior heads of 19 industrial organisations and management institutions stated that already they realized the need to have greater Self Control but ended willy-nilly trying to control others. What therefore, was required, the respondents felt, as to 'How to go about developing higher Self Control as a human value in work situations?' What started as a typical research work accordingly transformed itself into the researcher and the responding organisations 'working together 'on the task at hand.

When the Emeritus Fellowship study was over in 2002, the responding organisations felt that the work of inculcation of values started as part of the study should not stop. Accordingly, a voluntary organisation by the name *Spandan* (Heartbeat), Foundation for Human Values in Management and Society, was formed.

When the two studies were over and findings were discussed, the feedback from the academicians and practitioners was quite useful and insightful. Bengt Gustavsson, (Stockholm University, Sweden), an authority on Transcendental Organisation, offered three comments:

1. The concept is self supporting, and espoused by managers, but the most important aspect is, how it is enacted? "I believe, we need a global management community who are enacting ***Spandan*** values; we have enough of hypocrites" The point is well-taken.
2. The concept as used now seems to encompass all good values and as such it becomes non committing, or even empty. How does ***Spandan*** for example differ from God?, the concept we usually ascribe good values to.

   Values are by definition good and normative. The approach of *Spandan* is to enable the organisations and institutions identify those values considered suitable for them to achieve their missions and objectives more effectively.
3. About, 'Inculcating values'; the critical point is "in raising a management consciousness and associated action in tune with human values. It is NOT, I also believe sufficient with intellectual embracement of concepts, they have to be inculcated in the emotions, body and flesh of the manager and his organisation. But, how to do it.?"

   Any value, it is submitted, represents a strongly held positive attitude. Unless, therefore, a value or set of values considered desirable are strongly believed and adhered to, the purpose of inculcation cannot be achieved .Conscious, consistent and concerted efforts at propagation should therefore precede inculcation. Propagation, in its turn, should be preceded by top management and core group, "the executive wing" of the process of propagation and inculcation of human values in the given organisation, should be wedded to the philosophy of integrating values with work ethic and organisation culture. The assumptions and beliefs of *Spandan*'s approach are discussed in section 4.4 below; and the conditions necessary for effective inculcation of values are stated in chapter eight. One cycle of inculcation process takes around an year – after which the Core Group needs to keep it going in the role of the internal change agent.

The second feedback is from Pradeep Bhattacharya, a senior administrator interested in human values feels that inculcation of human values in an organisation should be mutually reinforcing with the institution of family and family values. He gives the example of Norway where family values play a critical role in nurturing managerial thinking and values.

The point is well-taken. Family with mother being the first socializing agent plays an important role. In a relations – oriented society like that of India, family values do assume critical role in nurturing managerial thinking and values. The success of Indians and settlers from India in various walks of life including entrepreneurship abroad is to a large extent the result of adherence of values in their family life and career. The breakdown of family system and traditional values in heralded, what is known as, the culture of acquisition in the West. It is in this context that the efforts of countries like Norway in strengthening family as an institution are to be viewed. The Prime Minister of Norway, for instance, has constituted a number of Commissions on rebuilding family values through corporate sector.

4.3 The Mission of *Spandan*

The missing of *Spandan* is propagation and inculcation of human values in management and society. *Spandan* attempts at offering an approach and process in facilitating educators and practitioners in management in striving for an optimal balance between Results and Relations as a means of developing a Functionally Humane Organisation.

4.4 Assumptions and Beliefs

In retrospect, we realize that *Spandan* owes its origin to certain assumptions and beliefs: **Assumptions**, equivalent to facts in most cases, are as follows:

1. That the relentless and obsessive pursuit of materialism by mankind resulted in an imbalance between materialism and spiritualism, results and relations; 'Steep profits and shallow relationships' – (Dalai Lama); 'swollen head' and 'shallow heart' (G.P. Rao 1996); and, (tall) men and (short) character'– (Dalai Lama);
2. That generally in all work situations it is more personal perceptions towards one's beliefs that one fails to understand the constraints of other person. This leads to the emergence of most of the problems in the organisation;
3. That the way out lies in restoring the lost balance through suitable efforts at values orientation in work situations and society;

4. That, such orientation of values consists of propagation and inculcation: propagation through teaching and research; and inculcation through training and facilitation (consultation). The process thus envelops management education and profession, and enjoins equal responsibility on both the thinkers and 'doers';
5. That in work situations, the 'challenge', and therefore, the opportunity – is how to work oneself, and make others work well (results) and importantly to make others work willingly (relations); and
6. That such an effective and optimal balance between results and relations leads to a good fit between bottom and top lines, *i.e.*, Productivity, Profitability and Employee commitment and belongingness.

Certain basic **beliefs** which spur the movements in values orientation are as follows:

1. That human beings are basically good; but, more often than not, represent divinity and devilry at the same time;
2. That human beings are capable of harnessing their divinity to the hilt through – in the ultimate analysis – self-realisation and activation; and
3. That when applied to work situation, a human being is capable of doing his best with proper leadership, motivation and communication.

4.5 The Approach and 3-D Process

Propagation of human values is done through teaching, research and training primarily by management educational institutions and trainers. Human Values can form integral part of the course curricula and learning processes of typical teaching programmes of duration of two/three years. Human values can form basis for doctoral theses. Tailor made seminar courses and workshops can be mounted and offered. The recipients would be management students, faculty, research scholars and T&D professionals, functionaries in management, administration and social service organisations.

Spandan is undertaking propagation on its own and through its Centre's for Human Values formed in collaboration with its Member Institutions.

Inculcation of human values in the given organisation is sought to be undertaken by a process called as 3-D Process of Diagnosis, Discovery and Development. The 3-D Process consists of identifying values by the organisation congruent to its Mission Statement and integrating them to its work ethic. The

Process is based upon Experiential Learning with Introspection and Feedback as its plank. The assumption and experience is that such an integration of values with work ethic enables the management to become, what I may submit, as 'functionally humane'.

4.6 The Impact

Assessing the effectiveness of training on human performance, productivity and satisfaction has always been 'a hard nut to crack' so to say. The difficulty is more so in the case of propagating and inculcating an apparently abstract concept like 'values'. N.R. Narayana Murthy, Chairman and Chief Mentor, Infosys, an organisation reputed for its value based management, responded to the question of measuring the effectiveness of values. Inciting, Infosys as an example. He said that, "The corporate social values of the company have undergone changes. The only way to assess the impact is the 'feeling' belonged and proud to be part of the organisation".

The component of feeling also has played an important role in measuring the impact of *Spandan* in its efforts of propagation in general and inculcation in particular of values, in context of groups and organisations. The impact of propagation of human values to prospective professionals has been found to be in terms of their increased awareness and consciousness of employees as human beings. In other words, they are mentally prepared to cope with unexpected and uncomfortable situations created by "others", in their career.

Propagation of human values to functioning professionals in management and administration gives them an opportunity to introspect and possible improvement in their future performance.

The impact of inculcation of human values through the 3-D process aims at humanising individual, workgroups and organisation concerned. The intended outcome, as stated earlier, is to develop **Functionally Humane Organisation**.

The characteristics of such an organisation have been found to be as follows:

1. Lessened misunderstandings;
2. Improved understanding of the behaviour of others;
3. Increased cooperative spirit and fraternity;
4. Mutual reinforcement of orientation of values;
5. Willingness to do one's best;
6. Greater resilience and flexibility;
7. Higher workgroup cohesiveness;

8. Better performance and increased productivity;
9. Higher employee pride, commitment and identification with the organisation; and
10. Sensitive and sympathetic appreciation of the difficulties faced by management during adversity like recession or a financial meltdown.

■ Better Performance and Increased Productivity (Characteristic – 8): An Illustration

Bangalore unit of Chandigarh based Kamala Dials and Devices Ltd., had undergone a series of *Spandan* workshop for over a period of 2 years. One such workshop was organized in April, 2004, with the objective of offering the management and organisation a direction in evolving work ethic in their unit. Several values were identified and decided to be adhered to. Dials unit, Hands Unit and Tool Room which comprised the company were assigned different targets.

Tool Room was assigned 'first time acceptance of component and tools' as one of its targets. The subsequent impact of the performance of tool room was recorded by the core group of the company as follows: "In that direction, beyond anybody's expectation, Mr. K.S. Sathyrnarayana, unit head – Tool room and his team with the consistent, quality and expert guidance of Mr. Raghavan, COO (S) proved their worth. It is also worth mentioning that their efforts have been well appreciated by one of our clients Deutsch Group, when the final approval of the '25020 – 2 Toggle Spring' got first time acceptance, though this component is considered to be one of the more difficult within the Relay Division of Deutsch Group. The group also expressed their feeling by writing, 'you and your group have clearly proven your abilities to handle such a tool'".

❑❑❑

5

The 'Humane' Side of Management: A Restrospective

> *Progress does not ultimately consist of merely industrial enterprises. That is only a symptom of it. Progress has ultimately to be measured by the quality of human beings – how they are improving, how their lot is improving, and how they are adopting themselves to modern ways and yet keep their feet firmly planted on their soil.*
>
> — **Jawaharlal Nehru**

Humanising management, as has been stated, denotes willingness and ability of management to integrate human values with Mission Statement and work ethic of the organisation by having an optimal balance between Results and Relations.

After having introduced ourselves with the concept of humanising management and the role of *Spandan* in the process, our effort in the present chapter would be to have a historical perspective of the concept. A perusal of economic history and industrial growth in India since 1850s when the process of industrialization started makes one feel that the management and industry has had so far gone through broadly four phases, and currently passing through the fifth phase in their endeavor of striking balance between Results and Relations. While the attempt has been done with India as the frame of reference, one tends to believe that at global level also the essence and sequence of the scenario may not be much different.

The historical perspective of humanising management and industry in India has been attempted by following the findings and the analytical framework of the classical work, Industrialism and Industrial Man by Clark Kerr and his colleagues (Kerr, Clark *et al.* 1960).

5.1 Management: Certain Perspectives

Clark Kerr, Frederich Harbison, Charles A. Myers and John T. Dunlop constituted the team, Inter University Study on Labour and Industrial Relations, and carried out several path-breaking research studies across the countries which yielded rich concepts, analytical frameworks, empirical data and far reaching insights. **The Industrialism and Industrial Man (1960)** is one such study.

A major finding of the International Study covering, among others, India has had been that the industrialization process across the world over a period of time has resulted in two broad and rather mutually incompatible trends. The first trend relates to the technological developments in the industry accompanied by corresponding breakthroughs in transport and communication services. This resulted in uniformity and homogeneity in production processes and in the methods of dealing with factors of production other than human beings. The second trend, relates to culture. Emanating from traditions and ethos of people living in a particular country, on the other hand, resulted in diversity and heterogeneity in workforce and their attitudes .Viewed from the standpoint of humanising management, technology is universal and more oriented towards **Results**; and, culture is situational and more congruent with **Relations.**

The analytical framework developed by Clark Kerr and his colleagues in this seminal work comes handy in understanding as to how management could and did cope with these challenges and availed the opportunities for blending hard and soft sides of human enterprise. Management has been viewed and analyzed from three standpoints: Management as a Resource; management as a Class; and, management as a System of Authority.

Management as a Resource is highly specialized and scarce; needs to be properly trained and developed; and, therefore, stands as a class by itself.

In India, management as a Resource remains scarce, in terms of its quality in particular, even after six decades of achieving freedom and after more than four decades of initiating National Policy on Management Education by establishing the first two Indian Institutes of Management in Ahmedabad and Calcutta in 1960.

Secondly, **Management as a Class** refers to the origin of managers from the particular segments (s) of the society, to which they belong. Kerr's survey at international level revealed that there were three major sources from where managers originate: **Patrimonial; Political; and, Professional**.

1. Management as a **Patrimonial class** arises when inheritance becomes the eligibility to enter and occupy even the highest position in an

organisation without requisite qualifications and experience. India and many other countries in East stand testimony to this class;

2. Management as **Political class** emerges when the political patronage and support enable a person to assume the roles of Chairman and Managing Director, typically in public sector undertaking and corporation. Countries belong to Communist Block are a prime example of the same; and,

3. Management as a **Professional class** refers to the induction of persons in an organisation based upon their qualifications and experience.

Thirdly, **Management as a System of Authority** denotes the manner in which decisions are taken by the management. Four possible situations are visualized: The first two when the management is the sole rule maker; and, the other two when the management has to share rulemaking with others. When the management has the monopoly of power, its attitudes to others – workers, in particular – could be of two types. One is that of authoritarianism. The leadership style and organisation culture make it clear that management has the 'prerogative' to rule. The other attitude is one of pity and sympathy. Philanthropy is the behavioural manifestation of such an attitude and has resulted in what is known as '*mai baap*' approach. Certain business communities like Parsees are well known for their labour welfare activities undertaken on their own without any legal requirement. It is, however, significant that the concept of philanthropy has undergone change in recent times. Philanthropreneurs, or philanthro capitalists, are young, first generation and highly successful entrepreneurs. They have passion to bring about social change with their money, time and skills. They believe that the benefits of capitalism which they have reaped can be applied to the service of charity. Warren Buffet and Bill Gates from abroad and Narayana Murthy, Azim Premji, Sunil Mittal and Kiran Mazumdar Shaw from India are some of the leading figures in the field.

When on the other hand the management is to share rule making with others like government and trade unions, its attitude could again be of two varieties. One, unwillingness and inability to accept workers as partners in decision making. This leads to legalistic or constitutional approach characterized by complying with the letter – rather than the spirit – of the law. The other possible attitude is one of willingness and ability to share the power with others. This results in democratic – participative approach.

Juxtaposing all the four possibilities as a continuum, we find

Sole Rule making________________________Sharing the rule making.

Authoritarian – Paternalistic — Legalistic – Democratic participative.

In a country like India with its (*a*) geographical vastness; (*b*) regional, economic, political and social variations and imbalances of a high order; and, (*c*) cultural diversities, all the four possible systems of authorities can be found operating. The attempt however would be to delineate broad contours and predominant trends phase wise.

5.2 Humanising Management In India: Certain Perspectives

■ Phase I: Initiation of Industrialization Process – Pre-World War I (1850s–1914)

RESULTS, RESULTS AND RESULTS

Industrial Revolution in the world commenced in the early-eighteenth century in England, moved to Europe, Americas and later to Asia and Africa. In India, the process of industrialization started during 1850's when cotton, jute, sugar, cement and paper industries came into being accompanied by plantation and mining. During the same period the first railway track was commissioned between Bombay and Thane, thereby signaling a revolution in transport system in the country. Excepting Tata Iron and Steel Company (TISCO) which commissioned its operations in 1904, the industry in India on the eve of the First World War in 1914 was in a nascent stage.

During this phase of commencement and consolidation of traditional manufacturing industries, the undivided attention of the industry was on efficiency, minimization of costs, reduction of waste and maximisation of profits. It was not a coincidence that the phase saw the emergence of Capitalism, Free Enterprise, '*laissez faire*', Scientific Management and Traditional Theories of Organisation. There was neither the felt need nor inclination to look at the human side of the enterprise. Results, in other words, held the centre stage. Relations, representing 'the humane face' of management was nowhere to be seen!

■ Phase II: Expansion and Growth – Changing Environment – First World War 1914–1918 – Second World War 1939–1945 – Formation of the United Nations 1945 – Attainment of Independence (1947) – 1914–1947

RESULTS VS. RELATIONS

Spiraling inflation, increasing cost of living, accumulating profits, amassing of wealth by a few, in contrast to abysmal poverty and misery by many sharpened the angst of downtrodden (industrial workers included) and sown seeds for militancy in all spheres of activity. Militant trade unionism, communism, industrial conflicts and resorting to violence were some the offshoots of such a volatile situation. All these developments forced the industrialists to adopt means to carry workers along with them rather than compelling and coercing them. Human Relations approach, paternalism, worker participation in management and industrial democracy were some of the methods adopted by management to develop harmonious industrial relations. Relations, in other words, were given importance rather reluctantly and grudgingly by unwilling employers. We must however at this point acknowledge the fact that certain business communities like Parsis were right from the beginning going voluntarily beyond the legal requirements of terms and conditions of employment. They adopted paternalistic approach in dealing with their workers and created loyal and productive workforce.

The formation of the United Nations Organisation (UNO), after the Second World War, in 1945 for establishment of peace and prosperity in the world is another milestone in bringing about a sense of equality and dignity in the downtrodden individuals, institutions, communities and countries. The only surviving agency of the League of Nations, formed after the cessation of hostilities in 1918, International Labor Organisation (ILO) has tripartite forum of organisation with government, industry and workers as equal partners. It adopted Conventions and Recommendations as means of improving the workers' lot and industrial relations across the world. The consequences, understandably, have been manifold: impetus to unionism, emergence of strong workforce, increased sense of self awareness, importance and dignity among workers. The employers in turn had to reorient themselves, their attitudes and their management styles to be in tune with the changing aspirations of the workers.

■ Phase III: Tardy Industrial Growth – State Regulation – Sheltered Markets (1947–1956)

Results vis a vis Relations

The first decade after the attainment of independence by India has been a transition. India after a long struggle got political Independence. Economic and Social Independences were yet to be attempted.

Reconciling the dictates of technology with the delicacy of humaneness became a new challenge and therefore an opportunity for management to deal with during this phase. The transition of managerial attitudes of this period resulted in the possible scenarios as visualized above in terms of management as a Resource, as a Class and as a System of Authority emerging in the country.

■ Phase IV: Industrial Policy Resolution Ii (1956) – Introduction Management Education – Accelerated Industrial Growth

Results and Relations

The Government of India adopted its second Industrial Policy Resolution in 1956 which laid emphasis on greater philip and decreased restrictions on industrial growth in the country. With increase in traditional manufacturing industries, emergence of modern and highly technological oriented industries, and with the tertiary sector comprising services industries, professionals in larger numbers and with newer skills were required

The need for larger number of professionals in management with newer capabilities had been anticipated by the government which declared its policy on management education. The first two Institutes of Management were established at Ahmedabad and Calcutta in early sixties – which were in due course increased to six as of now (2009); and plans to increase the number manifold in near future. Simultaneously, more and more scions of industrial groups and business communities were getting themselves educated and trained in management. As a consequence, the composition and complexion of the three facets of management started changing remarkably – towards the right ends of the continua.

■ Phase V: Privatization, Liberalization and Globalization – Sunrise Industries. Global Village – Cross cultural Management – (1991 and onwards)

Results through Relations

Although delayed, the Government's opening up of the Indian economy in 1991 turned out to be an epoch making event in the history of the country. The three pronged approach of privatization, liberalization and globalization enabled the Indian industry to show its mite both internally and externally: Internally – through consolidation, expansion and diversification; and, externally – through offering competition to the established world leaders in industry and business on their own turf, so to say. Emergence of Information Technology and IT enabling services entirely changed the contours of industrial map of the country. It brought in a new breed of professionals, virtual organisation, flexible work culture and vibrant lifestyles. The accompanying growth of transport communications and services industry gave further fillip to the process. As a result, the management and industry needed to have a fresh re-look at themselves at others and at their ways of motivation and leadership.

Corresponding developments were taking place in three facets of management, *viz.*, management as a resource, as a class and as a system of authority. As a resource, professional education in management has become accessible to larger and newer members of society. This happened because of expansion in management institutions in the country, government initiatives at making available professional education to larger and newer segments of society, and rising levels of aspirations due to increasing education, knowledge explosion, greater awareness and keener desire to rise in one's own life and career. Management as a class, accordingly, showed more and more incumbents in professional category, while patrimonial class also at the same time had its scion educated and professionally. Consequently, management as a system of authority started moving towards democratic participative approach. The cumulative effect of all these happenings and developments understandably **has had** to be positive in terms of felt need, initiation and implementation of the process of humanising management.

The 'seamy' side of Globalisation, in the meantime, started casting it shadows in the West in the second half of the 20th century with increasing ferocity and damage to the social, economic and cultural fabrics of the countries and societies therein.

Most of the current corporate efforts at humanising the organisation are concentrated on Corporate Social Responsibility (CSR). The concept of corporate governance is quite laudable and certainly an improvement over its earlier efforts like Social Responsibility of Business. CSR is necessary, but not sufficient. The reason is that present day codes of corporate governance are strongly anchored in the concept of fiduciary responsibility rather than moral responsibility. For transformation, business leaders will have to listen not merely to what analysts say the market expects of them, but to their own inner voices as well. It is therefore quite appropriate that Tomorrow's Company emphasizes that such transformation calls for "new measures of success, values and establishing new frameworks to create level playing fields." Tomorrow's Company was a Report prepared by the Think Tank for the Meeting of Business Leaders held in London in June, 2008.

The widely quoted Price Waterhouse global study, "Straight from the CEO" (1998), beautifully captured the same spirit when it proclaimed that CEOs of today wanted A , B and C: A (Awareness), B (Belief) and C (Conduct).

❑❑❑

6

The Systems Thinking: An Analytical Framework of the Study

> *Two eyes give us stereoscopic vision and along with two ears, depth perception. Is it not possible that, following the same design principle, reason and intuition are designed to work in harmony for us to achieve our potential intelligence? Systems thinking may hold a key to integrating reason and intuition.*
>
> *As managers gain facility with systems thinking as an alternative language, they find that many of their intuition become explicable. Eventually, reintegrating reason and integration may prove to be one of the primary contributions of systems thinking.*
>
> — **Peter M. Senge**

This chapter aims at developing an analytical framework based upon the viewing point of **Mother, Management,** *Spandan* **and Humanising Management.**

The purpose is to understand humanising management which has been defined as management attempting at transforming itself through suitable attitudes and values to become effective and humane at personal, professional, organisational, societal and cosmic levels.

6.1 Systems Thinking

The analytical framework is based upon systems thinking. Also known as systems approach and systems analysis, the purpose is to bring in a new perspective in understanding human behaviour. Its two cardinal principles are the principle of wholism and interdependence. Wholism refers to looking at an entity or issue in its entirety. Interdependence is as between and among the different components and constituents of the given entity or the issue. The concepts of supra system and subsystem become relevant. Supra system is larger entity and consists of smaller entity, or entities, called as sub systems. Organsiation for example is supra system and departments are its subsystem. The organisation, however, in its turn is subsystem of the society. When these subsystems are viewed as part of the given system, the concept of oneness emerges. An analogy is that of human body. Different limbs of a human body have their own features and functions. Yet the common objective of all the limbs is survival and growth of the human being.

Input – Transformation – Output is the other component in systems thinking. An entity exists for a purpose, objective or an aim (Output). To achieve the given objective(s), the entity obtains the required resources (Inputs) and uses them (Transformation) so as to achieve the given objective(s). Feedback, knowledge of results, becomes the mechanism for constant review and planning needed for the survival and growth of the given entity.

For a brief review of contributions on systems thinking and theory made by Fritzof Capra, Marshall McLuhan and Peter M. Senge are some of the pioneers of systems thinking and approach .A brief review of their contributions is presented as an endnote to the chapter.

6.1.1 Systems Thinking, Organisations and Humanising Management

When applied to organisation, it cane be noted that an organisation is a system by itself. It has its own objective (Output). It has its own resources- both human and otherwise (Input). It has and develops its own mechanism of using its resources to achieve the given objective(s) (Transformation). Finally, it has to keep itself together (Survival) and develop (Growth) through constant communication and interaction within and without (Feedback). The last two expressions of 'within' and 'without', bring out significantly the dimensions of subsystems and supra systems. Individuals at different levels with different social and cultural mileu and functioning in different departments and segments represent a significant dimension of 'within' and constitute its subsystems. The community, society, country, world and cosmos within which the given organisation functions represent the dimension of 'without' and constitute its supra systems.

When applied to humanising management, the relevance of systems thinking can hardly be exaggerated in view of the fact that humanising management by definition *is* transformation of human beings from a particular state (Lower self) to another desired state (Higher Self) at individual, professional, organisational and societal levels.

6.2 Analytical Framework

6.2.1 Input

■ Input: Environment – External

Environment for manager and management functioning in an organisation consists of extra organisational and intra organisational environment The environment outside the organisation can be viewed at two levels:

National Level: Environment where society, government and economy become supra systems of the given organisation. Some select external factors influencing the management at organisational level include: Economic Growth; Social Justice; and, development with 'human' face.

International Level: Globalisation has had been the pivot accompanied by Globality (management of globalization); Cross cultural management, requiring new sets of knowledge , skills and attitudes to deal with people located in units across the world with a variety of cultural mileu.

The impact of environment as an input on the functioning of management and its organisation can hardly be exaggerated. Government and society cause or allow the creation of an organisation, set its boundaries, lay down the rules of the game, act as the umpire and disciplinarian. The role and relevance of national level environment, in particular, permeates the entire functioning of the organisation – therefore the analysis of this work as a whole.

■ Input: Environment – Internal

The environment within the organisation can be viewed as consisting of sub systems. Kast and Rosenzweig in their work, Organisation and Management: A Systems and Contingency Approach (19), visualize five such subsystems:

- **Goals subsystems** refers to the objective(s) with which an organisation has been formed. Often stated through Mission Statement, the objectives become lodestar for its functioning.
- **Structural subsystem** involves the ways in which the tasks of the organisation are divided (differentiation) and coordinated (integration).
- **Technical subsystems** refers to the knowledge required for the performance of tasks, including the techniques used in the transformation of inputs into outputs
- **Psychosocial subsystem** consists of individual behaviour and motivation, status and role relationships, group dynamics and influence systems.

- **Managerial subsystem** spans the entire organisation by relating the organisation to its environment, setting the goals, developing comprehensive strategic and operational plans, designing the structure and establishing control processes.

6.2.2 Transformation and Output

■ Towards Self as a Human Being and as a Professional

Manager as a *Human Being*: Human Behaviour is considered as a function of Individual and Situation. Individual refers to the self. Personality, Learning, Perception, Motivation and Attitudes are some of the important concepts related to self. Situation refers to the environment surrounding influencing the given individual. As mentioned, Family, Community, Society, Industry and the Country constitute Situation or Environment to the manager. The means for transformation as a human being is through experiential learning consisting of introspection and feedback. Continuous interactions with all concerned help the manager achieve the desired balance between head and heart. Symbolically, it represents ascesnt from 'i '(lower self) to I (higher self).

Manager as a *Professional:* The relevant concepts are knowledge, skills and attitudes required by manager for performance at individual and institutional levels. He has to work (*a*) with and through work group at the same time, (*b*) with colleagues and seniors. Experiential learning sessions with the work group and others helps the manager to achieve the required balance between professional attachment while working and emotional detachment in not craving for reward. This balance is called as Karma Yoga Bhagawad Geetha. Symbolically, the progession is from 'I' (higher level) to 'we'(group identity).

■ Towards Organisation: Management is a Group of Professionals

Management is a group of *Professionals* is responsible for the functioning of an organisation. Managerial Transformation through human values at organisational level is achieved through the 3-D (Diagnosis, Discovery and Development) of *Spandan*. The objective of the process is to integrate values with work ethic as anchored to the mission statement of the organisation. The intended outcome is balance between **Results and Relations**. Symbolically, the movement is from 'we' (small group) to 'WE' (larger croup).

■ Towards the Society

The immediate supra system of an organisation is the society with the government as an important organ. The objective of a developing society such as India is to have balance between economical development and social justice.

The role of the management is to be an **O**rganisational **C**itizen (in contra distinction to **C**orporate **C**itizen) so that it helps the government achieve growth 'human face.' Symbolically the transformation is from 'WE' (larger group) to 'ours' (identity with society).

The preceding three responsibilities towards Self, Organisation and Society relates to managers functioning in their professional capacity. This is the **POINT OF VIEW** of the present work with the primary objective of offering a process for transformation at organisational level.

Moving beyond the management of organisations, we enter into dealing with (*a*) World and (*b*) Universe. The management as an identity merges itself with humanity as its part.

■ Management of the World

Assumes special significance in the context of ongoing globalization. Managing people with diverse nationalities and cultures is a challenge calling for cross cultural management. The two basic tasks here are:

1. Sustainable Development
2. Spiritual Democracy

The desired objective is balance between Technology and Culture. Symbolically the movement is from 'ours'(national identity) to 'O' (global identity). The east looks at it as *Vasudhaiva Kutumbakam* (Global identity).

■ Management of the Universe

The frame of reference here is the cosmos and task is balance between the mother earth and ecology. The transformation is through universal consciousness. Symbolically the ascent is from 'Ours' (Global identity) to theory of Oneness. No wonder, these days physicists are taking as vedic scholars.

This is the viewing point; and a pointer for mankind to reinvent their innate divinity to remake itself.

6.2.3 Insights and Issues

Transformation of management through human values is undertaken by two means; Propagation and Inculcation.

Propagation consists of teaching, research and training. The Indian ethos offer the insights for the transformation process. These are (*a*) Mother (empathy of highest order), (*b*) *Spandan* (heartbeat, vibration), (*c*) *Vasudhaiva Kutumbakam* (Global identity) and (*d*) Universal Consciousness.

The issues to be addressed are:

1. Integrating values with academics and through learning processes (KSA).
2. 'Teaching' values to prospective and functioning professionals
3. Education industry interface

Inculcation of human values at organisational level consists of enabling the management integrate values with work ethic as anchored to mission statement. The 3-D process of Diagnosis, Discovery and Development is adopted for the purpose for the organisation with *Spandan* as prime facilitator.

The issues to be addressed are:

1. How to translate the initial enthusiasm and admiration of the top management on human values into initiation of the process of inculcation in the organisation? (From Admiration to Administering);
2. How to translate awareness of values into adherence in one' life and career? (From Awareness to Action);
3. How one's adherence of values is to be manifested properly and perceived as such by others? (Possession, Projection and Perception);
4. What do we mean by Optimal balance between Results and Relations, which is considered as the sine qua non of effective inculcation of values in the given organisation? (Optimality in balancing Results with Relations).

The first issue is dealt with in chapter eight (8.12); and, the remaining three in chapter nine.

6.2.4 FEEDBACK

The fourth and last component of systems approach is Feedback. Feedback consists of constant monitoring, reviewing and initiating timely corrective actions. Based upon the outcomes of humanising management at individual, professional, organisational and societal levels, suitable modifications and improvements are to be initiated in the transformation process.

Humanising Management: Transformation Through Human Values – An Analytical Framework

INPUT

International
- Globalization
- Globality
- Cross Cultural Management
- Human Dignity

↕

National
- Economics Growth
- Social Justice
- Development with Human Face

↕

Organisational (Subsystems)*
- Goals Subsystems
- Structural Subsystems
- Technical Subsystems
- Psychosocial Subsystems
- Managerial Subsystems

→

TRANSFORMATION

Entity/Unit	Level	Means of Transformation
Manager as a Human being	Individual	Experiential Learning – Introspection – Feedback
Manager as a Professional	Work Group	Focal Person-Work Group Interactive events
Management and Organisation	Organisation	*Spandan* 3-D Process
Management and Society	Society	Organisational Citizenship
Management and Globalisation	World	Sustainable Development
Management and Universe	Cosmos	Spiritual Democracy [Vasudhaivaka Kutumbam]

→

OUTPUT

Nature of Balance	Symbolic Representation
Between Head and Heart	i to I
Between Professional Attachment and Emotional Detachment [Karma Yoga]	I to We
Between Results and Relations	we to We
Between Economic Development and Social Justice	We to ours
Between Technology and Culture	ours to Ours
Between Earth and Ecosystem	Ours to Oneness

FEEDBACK/FEED FORWARD

Endnotes

Some of the Classic Works on Systems Thinking

Capra, McLuhan and Senge have laid foundation for systems thinking and theory and its application to understanding the different facets of human behaviour. Fritzof Capra. (The Tao of Physics, 19), the founding director of the Centre for Ecoliteracy in Berkeley, California, US developed the 'Science of Quality as a science of relationships'; "From the beginning of western science, there have been two schools of thought: one that focuses on the study of matter or quantities, and the other on pattern and quality. Though dominated by the former, branches of science that emerged in the 20th century, like systems theory, cybernetics, quantum physics and ecology, focus on quality or pattern.

One proposes a synthesis of these two approaches through a conceptual framework that integrates the biological, cognitive and social dimensions of life. A science of quality is a science of relationships." (Interview, *Times of India*, March 5, 2008.) As his present status indicates, Capra's involvement in the understanding of relationships is now extended to the relationship of human beings with the environment in the form of ecoliteracy. This aspect will be dealt with in the chapter on management and environment.

According to Marshall McLuhan (The Global Village: Transformation in Worldlife and Media in the 21st century, OUP, 1989), "the entire world was in the grasp of a vast material and psychic shift between the values of linear thinking of visual proportional space, and that of the values of the multi-sensory life, the experience of acoustic space. Culturally what was happening now is titanic. It needs a completely new frame of reference" (Preface). McLuhan offers simultaneous understanding or "integral awareness" as a key to understand both systems, *i.e.*, Western values of visual space and the oriental values of acoustic space, simultaneously. McLuhan's contribution to Global Village in terms of tetrad will be discussed in the chapter later.

Peter M. Senge, another legendary thinker (The Fifth Discipline: The Art and Practice of the Learning Organisation, Double day Currency, 1990), develops Bilateralism as a design principle underlying the evolution of advanced organisms. He then examines the efficacy of systems thinking in enhancing the managerial effectiveness. "Two eyes give us stereoscopic vision and along with two ears, depth perception. Is it not possible that, following the same design principle, reason and intuition are designed to work in harmony for us to achieve our potential intelligence?. Systems thinking may hold a key to integrating reason and intuition....

"As managers gain facility with systems thinking as an alternative language, they find that many of their intuition become explicable. Eventually, reintegrating reason and integration may prove to be one of the primary contributions of systems thinking." (pp.168-169)

❑❑❑

PART II

Spandan (Heartbeat, Vibration): Approach and Process

Part II on *Spandan* has three chapters, chapters seven to nine. These deal with the two major methods of transformation, namely Propagation (**Chapter** 7) and Inculcation (**Chapter 8**) of human values. The last chapter, **Chapter 9**, examines the insights and issues emanating from the process of inculcation of human values in management.

7

Propagation of Human Values: Insights and Issues

> *You cannot teach a man anything. You can only help him find it within himself.*
>
> — **Galelio, Galiei**
>
> *The whole purpose of education is to turn mirrors into windows.*
>
> — **Sydney J. Harris**

7.1 Value Based Management and Management Education

Having acquainted ourselves with the basic goodness of human being as the pivot of management of organisations, let us have a look at what is it that we want to do. The immediate objective is to enable the management develop a functionally human organisation characterized by an optimal balance between **R**esults and **R**elations. For developing such an organisation management has to subscribe and adopt values based management as its credo. Value based management, in essence involves humanising management at individual, professional and organisational levels such that the organisation as a whole becomes value oriented. The job of management education is to facilitate the management fraternity develop required knowledge skills and attitudes to become value based in their thinking communication and conduct. Since management education is professional education in its nature, the involvement of the profession concerned, *i.e.*, management, becomes *sina quo non* of the success of management education in achieving its objective. The Management education and management profession have to work *in tandem*. A functional and harmonies Education – Industry interface thus becomes the key for orientation of human values in management and the industry. Such orientation consists of Propagation and Inculcation of Values.

Propagation of values is primarily meant for prospective professionals. It involves teaching and research as the primary basis. Inculcation of human values is meant for functioning professional as the target group. The basic ingredients are training and consultancy in the form of facilitation. It is important to know that when put together, teaching, research, training and consultancy become a continuum. Further, teaching and research, *i.e.*, Propagation is the responsibility of management education. Training and consultancy on the other hand, are essentially professional oriented. In any case both the management institutions and industrial and other organisations have to be partners throughout. It is known that the industry participation in the education process is as important as the participation of education in the inculcation of values in the industry. These ideas are presented in Fig. 7.1 below:

Management Education		**Management Profession**
Teaching ⟷ Research	⟷	Training ⟷ Facilitation
Propagation of Human Values	⟷	Inculcation of Human Values
Spandan Approach	⟷	*Spandan* 3-D Process
(Faith in basic goodness Development of Human Being)	⟷	(Diagnostic, Discovery and Developmnet through experiential learning)

Spandan **Philosophy**
(Innate Divinity in Human Beings**)**

Fig. 7.1 Management Education – Industry interface and Human Values in Management

7.2 The Framework

Bases upon the experiences gain after the formation of *Spandan* in 2001, an analytical framework was developed to include the essential features of *Spandan* Approach and processes of propagation and inculcation.

7.2.1 The Issue

The ever eluding mirage like challenge facing mankind particularly at institutional level has been as to how best to have that 'magical' balance between **Head & Heart** and **Results & Relations.** The Challenge – and therefore the opportunity-is how to work oneself well and make others work **well** (Results) and how to work oneself **well** and **willingly** and make other work **well** and

willingly (Relations). The on going concern world over in management profession and education is a case in point. The concerned about renewing the felt need to 'correct' the rather skewed overemphasis on Results and bring in a greater element of Relations in the work ethic and organisational culture. As a consequence, the task for management education system is to reorient itself.

1. **Objective:** Graduating from an institute to an institution.
2. **Concepts:** With suitable emphasis on attitudes and values, *vis-a-vis* knowledge and skills.
3. **Mode-Propagation and Inculcation of Values:** Moving from teaching to enabling the students and practitioners learn through their experiences with introspection and feedback as its planks.

7.2.2 The Task

Objective: For an 'outfit' offering management education to graduate from an MBA institute to that of a Management institution would mean change in three respects:

(*i*) Greater balance between and among the four pillars of management education, *viz.*, teaching, research, training and consultancy

(*ii*) Due balance between and among the mixes of Knowledge (K), Skills (S) and Attitudes (A); and

(*iii*) Equal importance for enabling the students develop well rounded personalities with vision rather than stopping at making them effective competitors in the rat race of job markets.

7.2.3 Concepts

With reference to the concept of having better balance between Results and Relations at academic and professional levels, it is submitted that the contribution of Indian ethos and culture could be of significance. The three such important contributions could be (*i*) Maternalistic Management (The concept of Mother as symbolic of management philosophy); (*ii*) '*Karma Yoga*' (Professional attachment and Emotional detachment); and, (*iii*) '*Spandan*' (Vibration – indicating a high degree of sensitivity, arising out of conviction care, concern and compassion which are the cardinal attitudinal variables of Mother).

7.2.4 Mode

Propagation and inculcation of values

Instruments for Propagation and Inculcation of Human Values

No.	Theme	Objective	Duration	Target Group(S)
(A) Propogation*				
1.	Orientation Session	Introducing *Spandan* and its Objectives	Three to four hours	Homogeneous group
2.	Preview Workshop	Introducing 3-D Process of Inculcation of Human Values in an Organisation	Fourteen to sixteen Hours	Heterogeneous group
3.	Simulated Workshops	Introducing 3-D Process of Inculcation of Human Values in an Organisation – anchored to its Mission Statement	Fourteen to sixteen hours	Homogeneous group, *i.e.*, from the given organisation
4.	Seminar Course	Focus on the methodology of the Values inculcation process	Thirty hours	Homogeneous group, *i.e.*, participants from Academia, or, from Practitioners
B. Inculcation				
5.	Process of Values Inculcation	Facilitating the given organisation go through one cycle of the inculcation process with core group as the Internal facilitator	– 30 interactive days spread over 3–4 months with *Spandan* as co-facilitator (Initial Cycle) – Continuing the process through Core Group with *Spandan* as an external facilitator (ongoing)	The Organisation as a whole

* Along with *Spandan*, Propagation is also undertaken by its centers for Human Values established in collaboration with the Institutional Members

7.3 Propagation of Human Values

Propagation deals with the mode, delivery system or learning technology of human values in management. The human values cannot be 'taught' the way, for example, knowledge and skills are taught either by a teacher in a classroom or by a practitioner to his subordinates in a work situation. The only means available to the teacher and the superior is his actions conduct and ethical behaviour-the assumption being that the student and the subordinates' learn' about the appropriate values through the action or experience transmitted by, their teacher and mentors respectively. Thus, experiential learning based on introspection and feedback comes out as a potent means of transmitting and inculcating suitable human values in an education system and practising world.

7.3.1 Simulated Workshops/Seminars (No. 3 in above table) on

Select Aspects of Human Values, Work Ethic, Culture and Organisational Effectiveness (6 to 8 hours/12 to 16 hours)

Suggested Themes: As Emanating from the Empirical Evidences, Professional Experiences and Organisational Experiments the following are some of the major themes and perspectives for further analyses:

1. 'Swollen Heads and Shallow Hearts' Values orientation- Reinventing Ourselves
2. Results through Relations
3. Mission Statement, Human Values and Corporate Culture.
4. Prime Responsibility and Role Clarity for smoother functional relationship
5. Self-control and Managerial Effectiveness
6. Creativity, Employee Development and Performance
7. Empathy and Interdepartmental Cooperation
8. Service Orientation and Customer Satisfaction
9. Trust, Delegation and Employee Commitment
10. Fairness, Equity and Employee Commitment
11. Human Values and Organisational Strategy
12. Human Values and Organisational Culture
13. Organisational Culture and Change Management
14. Organisational Synthesis and Synergy through Managerial Transformation

15. Strategic Alternatives (Mergers / Acquisitions /Joint Ventures/ Takeovers) and Cross Cultural Management
16. Conflict Resolution, Change Management and Organisational Adaptation
17. Values Orientation and Stress Management
18. Relevance of Human Values in Transnational Management
19. Orientation of Values and Employee Identification during Crisis.

7.3.2 *Spandan*

Seminar Course (No. 4 in the above table) on Inculcation of Human Values in an Organisation (Contact Hours: 30), G.P. Rao (Founder Chairman, *Spandan*).

1. **Human Values in Management:** The Context: Global and National Scenario-Responses by the actors concerned, *viz.*, practitioners, institutional builders, academicians, policy makers and NGOs.
2. ***Spandan* at Interpersonal Level:** Maternalistic Management: The concept and it's application – Responses and reactions – Task ahead.
3. ***Spandan* at Institutional Level:** Balance between Results and Relations – Work ethic and organisational Culture – Indian Insights and experiences.
4. **Diagnosis:** Identification of suitable Human values through introspection and feedback based on Experiential Learning.
5. **Discovery:** Assessment of Human Values identified as above in the given organisation(s) through Experiential learning.
6. **Development:** Value orientation and Inculcation based on the proceeding identification and assessment of Human Values.
7. ***Spandan* at Cosmic Level:** Advaita Philosophy – Environmental management system and Eco-protection – Holistic and Spiritual orientation.
8. **Human Values in Management:** The future – Global and national scenario – Experiments at building value oriented organisation – Tasks ahead

7.4 Inculcation of Values (No. 5 in the Table)

The process of evolving such work ethic and organisation culture consists of three phases:

1. **Diagnosis:** Identifying suitable values congruent to the objective (s) of the given organisation.
2. **Discovery:** Assessing the extent to which the values thus identified are adhered to at a given point of time, and,
3. **Development:** Thinking of ways and means of strengthening the values thus diagnosed and discovered over a period of time. All these phases, it may be reiterated are to base on experiential learning of the members of the given organisation as a whole.

The *Spandan* 3-D Process is discussed in detail in later chapters.

7.5 The Framework as a Backdrop: Insights and Issues

Spandan, and The International Management Institute (IMI), New Delhi, (2006) organized a seminar on the theme of Values Based Management using the framework as its basis.

The objective of the process of graduating from 'an institute' to 'an institution', would involve a balance between:

- Teaching, research, training and consultancy
- The mixes of knowledge, skills and attitudes
- Capabilities to develop students intellectually as well as emotionally to become well-rounded individuals
- Vision and competitiveness

The three basic **concepts** constituting the bed rocks of human values in management were recommended for further chiseling and experimentation.

Suggestions were offered on the **mode,** which are as follows:

1. Human Values should be interwoven into the course curriculum. All functional subjects such as Finance, Marketing, Operations, HRD etc. must contain a perspective of values. A elective course on Human Course can be included in the curriculum which could be voluntary and non-credit. Functional specialization of Human Values can also be incorporated, depending on the availability of faculty and student interest.
2. Summer training and project reports.
3. Articles on real work situations from leading newspapers, websites and journals should be discussed, in the classroom.

4. CD's of speeches by respected business leaders on the role of values in management should be shown to the students and facilitation done through discussions.
5. Intensive workshops should be organised with leading successful professionals. Cases, role plays, simulation exercises could be prepared and given to the students.
6. Suitable human values could be identified with the help of organisations where the students are likely to be eventually placed. Feedback could be collected from students and their organsiations guides after they are placed regarding the value orientation programme.
7. Eminent persons from the industry, administration and other walks of life to be invited to interact with the faculty and students.
8. Most important, the faculty needs to behave as role models for the students.

❑❑❑

8

Spandan 3-D Process of Inculcation of Human Values

> *True knowledge is application.*
>
> — Goethe
>
> *We believe that the essence of success in business lies in developing vision and values, and embodying them in planning, managing and decision making.*
>
> — Kenneth Blanchard et al.

8.1 *Spandan* 3-D Process

8.1.1 The Objective and the Process

This chapter relates to introducing the 3-D Process of inculcation of values in an organisation. The objective is to:

(*a*) have Mission Statement of the organisation as anchor and

(*b*) weave the values in work fabric

(*c*) through experiential learning and

(*d*) integrating the values with HRD and Strategic Management for

(*e*) achieving an optimal balance between Results and Relations as a means for

(*f*) developing a Functionally Humane Organisation.

This process, it may be reiterated, is part of humanising management of organisations (Point of View) and igniting innate divinity in human beings for 'remaking ourselves' (Viewing Point).

A. Mission Statement as the Anchor

The role of human values is to enable the management achieve the objective of the organisation as best as possible. The mission statements assume accordingly importance in the process of inculcation of values. Further, there is an apprehension that values involve more of preaching, with renunciation mode so that a organisation may go astray when it tries to inculcate values in the system. When it is stated that it is the mission statement which determines the nature and extent of weaving values within the work fabric, such apprehensions are likely to be minimized. Whenever, therefore, an organisation decides to adopt the *Spandan* 3-D process, the mission statement to be adopted, if it is for the first time, or revisited if already in existence. The first box in the analytical frame work is the Mission Statement.

B. Weaving the Values in Work Fabric

After the mission statement either adopted or revisited, the management or core group would access the extent to which the objective of the organisation is achieved. Next, in order to improve upon, the accomplishment of the statement the role of values would be examined. There are three steps in the process:

■ Diagnosis

The management or core group would access the relevance of the 42 values included in the spectrum of values in work situation and would pick up the relevant values. There is no hard and fast rule on the number of values to be chosen. The purpose is to (*a*) keep balance between the values oriented to results and relation; (*b*) to chose an optimal number (normally between 6 -10) and ; (*c*) so that the purpose is clear to the members of the organisation as a whole.

After identifying the given number of values, three exercises are undertaken.

1. Defining, describing or giving a meaning to each value.
2. To operationalise each value in terms of behavioural manifestations and performance parameters.
3. To identify, the possibly undesirable consequences of improper, injudicious and inadequate or excess adherence to the value concerned.

As an illustration of how values can be defined by the core group based upon experiential learning, the set of 6 values identified and defined by **IDS Infotech Co. Ltd., Chandigarh, India,** is presented in BOX 8.1.

BOX 8.1 ***Spandan*** **3-D process: Identification and definition of human values by IDS Infotech Co. Ltd., 2006.**

Creativity: The ability of people to develop new ways and being innovative in identifying opportunities and solve problems so that we can provide better services to customers and employees to their satisfaction and success, and enhance the business opportunity for the organisation. Creativity is the art of coming out with something new or different using ones imagination and intelligence for performing the same task in an improved manner.

Commitment: Practising and adhering to one's own set of rules, roles and duties to a course of action which can be seen in sincerity and dedication towards ones own work and dedication. It also to honor the promises made to customers, employees and society all the time.

Customer Demand/Orientation: It means that the customer should be satisfied, delighted, understood and convinced. We should understand the customers needs and deliver the output with 100% quantity and quality so that the customer is successful in his objective of coming to IDS in all aspects.

Employee Orientation: A focus to develop happy employees into future leaders by training, recognizing the good performance and by creating an environment of trust, work and equal opportunities. It should also focus on providing the right environment for economic, social growth and quality of life to all the employees in the organisation.

Prosperity: A state of growing economically and infrastructurewise and making the clients, employees and shareholders proper year after year. It is also a state of happiness and self-motivation.

Competition: A drive to excel as compared to others and be ahead of others in industry and society by delivering best services and making employees satisfied etc.

The document containing, the list of values identified with their definition, operationalisation and precautions is circulated and feedback solicited from all the members of the organisation.

The core group would finalise the task of diagnosis, keeping in view the feedback received.

■ Discovery

This relates to assessing, the nature and extent of adherence to the values thus identified at individual, work group and organisation levels. The feedback is obtained and is used for having a picture of the extent of adherence at the different levels.

■ Development

Refers to the steps to be undertaken to improve upon the level of adherence. Basic documents would be prepared by the core group and feedback is sought. The plan of action is prepared thereafter.

C. The Self and Experiential Learning

The ***Spandan*** approach and 3-D Process of inculcation of values has been – and still is – evolving. The bedrock of the approach and the process is self – self awareness, self awakening and self actualisation at individual, professional and organisational levels. This is the rationale for Experiential Learning which employs introspection and feedback for the purpose. Experiential Learning is just the obverse of Participant Observation wherein the participants have the enviable task of participating in the discussions and deliberations 'intellectually' and animatedly and yet be able to observe and assess their own sentiments, interactions and activities as objectively as possible. In the oriental tradition it is known as Witness Approach.

D. Integrating the values with HRD and Strategic Management

■ HRD

Inculcation of select values is necessary but not sufficient. The values and their adherence must be linked to other related HRD functions.

The first such function is 'Selection'. While choosing persons for employment – at senior levels and at certain critical positions in particular, care should be taken that persons with right mindset and proper attitudes get selected. As rightly observed by Peter Drucker, the damage done by an dishonest manager to the organisation is more grievous than caused an incompetent manager.

The second HRD function is 'Training and Development'. The entire mechanism of the process is to be made part of the induction programme. Workshops are to be held on the 3-D process when the process of inculcation is started. Interactive sessions are to be held with eminent persons in the related fields. Core group members and others are to be sent for training and development at appropriate places and in appropriate areas.

The third HRD function is 'Performance Appraisal'. When incorporated with select values as the parameters of appraisal, the appraisal system becomes a powerful tool for motivation.

The fourth HRD function is Managerial Succession. A well-planned managerial succession and career planning will go a long way in attracting and retaining the persons with caliber and integrity to have a long term career with the organisation.

The fifth sphere of activity relating to HRD is rather subtle but significant. This refers to the ambiance, the social culture, the informal atmosphere as an important feature of the organisational life. To bring home the point, an experience may be related. The Chairman and Managing Director of a large organisation built it single handedly, was respected – almost revered by one and all. During the interviews with even the senior functionaries of the organisation, a very interesting set of responses were emanating. They said, they respected the CMD – only from a distance. They felt that his participation in family activities and social functions would go a long way in developing nearness to him and the company.

At the final meeting, after a series of workshops on the inculcation were over, the CMD was communicated of this feeling and perception towards him. The immediate and spontaneous response of the CMD was, "professor, it is an eye opener for me". Creating situations for informal get together as an ongoing process are found to be effective in developing *bon homie* in the company.

■ Strategic Management

Since the process of inculcation started with the mission statement, the end should be with the linked to the Strategic Management of the company. In other words, all the energies and resources are to be geared towards completion of the process, keeping in view the long term goals of the company.

E. Optimal Balance between Results and Relations

The spectrum of human values in work situation contains 44 values. These values can be categorized in terms of rules and regulations. Results relate to task orientation and are organisation specific. Some examples of such values are Profits, Customer Orientation and Shareholders claims.

Relations refer to social, emotional function and are people individual specific. Some examples of such values are fairness, employee needs and compassion.

There are certain values which are difficult to categories, because they are more or less, equally organisational specific and individual oriented. Some examples of such values are Creativity, Commitment and Discipline.

While selecting the values, care needs to be taken to have an optimal balance between and among such values.

F. Functionally Humane Organisation

The culmination of preceding steps and processes is to develop Functionally Humane Organisation**.** Functionally refers to results and task function. Humane relates to relations and to Social- emotional function. A balance between head and heart in the management and the organisation is thus the ultimate objective

8.1.2: Conditions Necessary for the Process to be Effective

■ Top Management Role and Support

Since Inculcation of values is to (*i*) envelop the entire members of the given organisation, (*ii*) be a continuous process, and (*iii*) to be anchored to the mission statement and to be integrated with the HRD and other policies and practices, the role of the top management becomes very critical.

While lack of top management support is a limitation, too much support is also equally to be avoided. When, in other words, rank and file feel that the process of inculcation of values is the 'baby' of the top management, or management, to that extent the total commitment and involvement of one and all – which is *sine qua non* of an effective change process – may get eroded and limited.

The experience revealed that eliciting required commitment from top management for the value orientation process lasting for several months was not quite encouraging. While they are appreciative of the concert of values and aware of the need to make their organisation enriched with suitable values, they appeared not to be able to spare sufficient time for interactive sessions with them and their senior colleagues.

After initiating the process, any compelling issue needing the attention of top management or requiring their presence elsewhere – mostly abroad – would make their availability for attending the monthly Core Group meetings difficult.

Further, it is observed, that the initial novelty and euphoria of experimenting with an important idea and transformational process may not be exciting over a period of time. This again, results in the reduced interest and involvement of the top management in the process.

■ Core Group

Core Group plays a very critical role in the process. A small, committed and competent group of functionaries representing the different segments of the organisation constitute the core group. It has, however not always been an easy task for the top management to constitute the group to their satisfaction. First, the limitation applicable to top management also apply-in varying degrees-to the members of core group as well – *viz.*, ensuring that the value orientation is not perceived as 'the baby' of the top and senior management; making them available to attend and participate in the core group meetings; and, sustaining the momentum of the process at an even and consistent level over a period of time.

In addition, Core Group members as also other senior functionaries-may have feeling that their participation in ***Spandan*** meetings and undertaking field work of values interferes in their own duties and responsibilities.

A more daunting task, however, is to create and maintain team spirit among the core group members and harness the same for the achievement of the stated objective of the odyssey, *viz.*, creating an optimal balance between results and relations.

8.1.3 Inculcation of Human Values in a given Organisation

Mission Statement – Diagnosis- Discovery – Development- Outcome.

- □ **Objective and Duration:** Human Values anchored to Mission Statement of the given organisation enveloping Selection , Appraisal, Training and Development and Organisation culture and Commitment in its gambit. Seven to Nine weeks, involving 16 to 20 contact days with ***Spandan*** as Facilitator to complete one cycle of inculcation of Human Values.

- □ **Process:** The process involves 3-D approach consisting of Diagnosis, Discovery and Development and is based on Experiential learning. Core Group plays the role of Executive Arm, conductor of research: Advisor to top management and as the change agent subsequent to the completion of the task of ***Spandan*** as a Facilitator of the given cycle of inculcation.

- □ **Ongoing Activity:** Core Group with ***Spandan*** visiting periodically to continue the process, which is a ever continuing activity.

Exhibit 8.1 ***Spandan*** **3-D Process – Sequencing**

Phases and Focus	Description of Activities	Catalyst(s)	Period Involved	*Spandan* Interation
1	2	3	4	5
I. Diagnosis	1. Mission Statement (Revisited if already Existing) 2. Selection of Suitable Human Values 3. Operationalisation	Top Mgmt, Core Group, *Spandan* " "	1-2 days 1-2 days 1-2 days -	1-2 days 1-2 days 1-2 days
		I	3 – 6 days	3 – 6 days
II. Discovery	1. Organisation wide survey on assessment (discovery) & suggestions (development) 2. Finalization and analysis of survey data	Core Group Core Group	2 -3 Weeks 1 – 2 Weeks	
		II	3 – 5 Weeks	
III. Development	1. Presentation of survey data on discovery and development 2. Discussion 3. Strengthening human values selected 4. Evolving/integrating complimentary policies and programmes on selection, appraisal, training & development org. culture and commitment			
		III	3 – 5 Days	3 – 5 Days
IV. Training and Development	1. Workshops on Human Values Selected 2. Focal Person Based Discovery and Development Sessions	Top Mgmt, Core Group, *Spandan* Top Mgmt, Core Group, *Spandan*	5 Days 5 Days	5 Days 5 Days
		IV	10 Days 7 - 9 Weeks	10 Days 16 – 20 Days
V. Implementation	1. Organisation-wise Conduct of Sessions and Workshops on Select Human Values 2. Execution of Intigrated Policies and Programmes (Iii-4)	Core Group Core Group, Top Mgmt	Ongoing 2 -3 months	
VI. Periodic Review and Planning	—	Top Mgmt, Core Group, *Spandan*		1 – 2 Days a Month

Spandan: **Inculcation of Human Values Anchored to Mission Statements and Obtaining Optimal Balance between Results and Relations.**

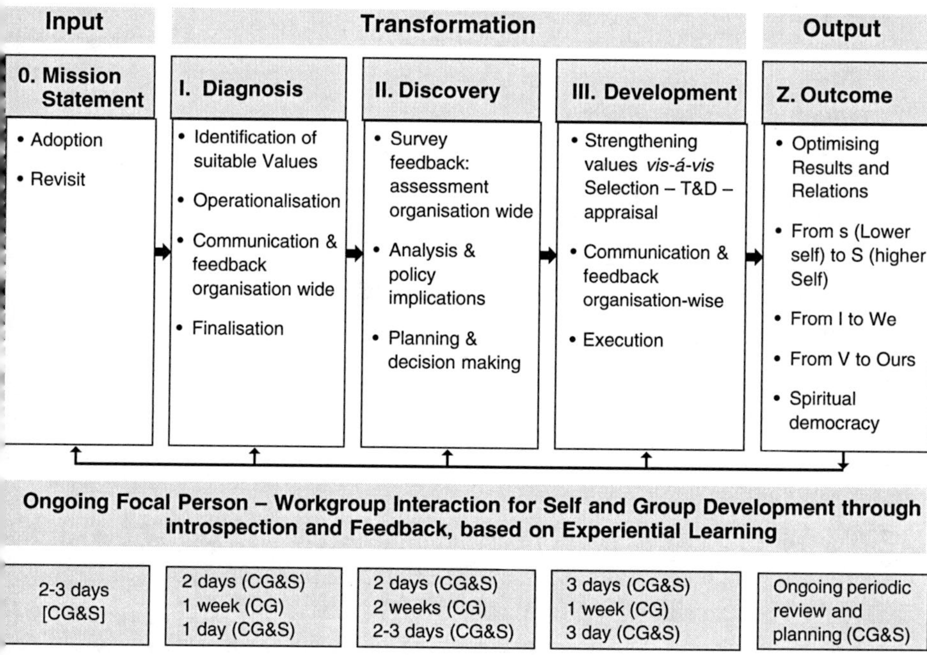

CG: Core group: Head of Institution, Chairman: 8-10 members, representing the different segment; and HRD/any other as Convenor.
S: *Spandan*: Facilitator.

With a view to after an idea as to how *Spandan* 3-D Process workgroups take place, an Appendix is incorporated to the chapter.

8.2 Similar Approaches and Practices

8.2.1 Management by Objectives (MBO)

MBO has had been highly popular as a Management Philosophy, Approach, by thinkers and academicians and was implemented by organisations throughout the world, including India, during mid 20th Century.

Peter F. Drucker, doyen on management thinking and a proponent of MBO described it as ‘more than a slogan, more than a technique, more than a policy even. It is so to speak a constitutional principle’. He adds that, “the MBO rests on a concept of the job of management. It rests on an analysis on the specific needs of management group and the obstacles it faces. It rests on a concept of human action, behavior and motivation. Finally, it applies to every manager, whatever his level and function, and to any organisation whether large or small. It insures performance by converting objective means into personal goals. This is a genuine freedom". The three characteristics of MBO are: (1) Participative Decision Making; (2) Goal setting and (3) Objective feedback (Drucker, Peter F. 1974).

The conditions required for implementation of MBO are as follows (Neil Miller):

- Full involvement of Board
- Commitment of and practised by CEO
- Common understanding of values
- Incorporation of Values in Management process
- Management not the judge of its own success and
- Values *viz-á-viz* remuneration

The MBO and the ***Spandan*** 3-D Process, are, as can be noted are very much similar in their philosophy, approach and process. S.K. Chakraborty, once a proponent of MBO in India had therefore rightly described the MBO as left brain rationalistic approach.

The MBO however did not continue effectively for long because of the very reason, that it confined itself to the left brain rational analytic. Chakraborty states: "Over succeeding years, through an extensive range of organsiational studies, it struck me that despite the range of elegant, rational, systematized analytic approaches employed – MBO included – neither effective and concrete organisational results, nor a wholesome and humane quality of work life had become manifest in India. It gradually began to dawn on me that the problem lay substantially in the weaknesses afflicting the sphere of human values". Chakrabory S.K. (199.).

S.K. Chakraborty, it may been noted, has subsequently become a pioneer in the movement of human values in management education and profession in the country.

8.2.2 The TATA Experiences and Practices

The TATA group has introduced two important landmark features in its functioning with a view to integrate values with its management structure. These are:

- The JRD Quality Values (QV Award)
- The TATA Unify HR Approach

■ The JRD Quality Values (QV Award)

It was started in 1995 as "A Process of ensuring quality – not of product or produce or performance alone – beginning with the people who work in the company and naturally ending, without any insincere protests to the contrary at the bottom line mentioned above". The group Chairman of the company Ratan Tata, described the award as a means of measurement of corporate leadership. The Award confines to the TATA group's 80+ companies, controlling among themselves over 2% of Indian industry.

■ The TATA Unify HR Approach

In the past, group heads of HR restricted their activities to co-ordinating and sharing information across business units. The group companies had its own HR policies and practices.

The TATA group, have introduced in 2002 a unified Human Resource's framework. For the purpose six divisions have been formed to handle crucial HR functions: (1) TATA Administrative Service (TAS), (2) Talent Management, (3) Management Development, (4) Programme Management, (5) Learning and (6) Research.

Explaining the implication of this reorganisation in HR, Satish Pradhan, Head of The TATA Unify HR Approach, states that, 'clearly there was an understanding within the group that there is a need to have a unified approach to HR rather than a uniform approach'.

8.2.3 The Turnaround of Indian Bank, 2008

An interesting example of undertaking a major Organisation Development (OD) initiative to ward off crisis relates to Indian Bank. The bank was declared inefficient in 1999 and Confideration of Indian Industry (CII) special committee recommended its closure. Ranjana Kumar, took over as the banks Chairman and MD in 2000. During her tenure, the bank was restructured and a few years later, it became one of the top two performing, public sector banks.

Ranjana Kumar, declared as India's turn around Queen, by The Economist records her experiences in the book, 'The Turnaround Story of Indian Bank'. Her basic assumption was that since the country was already riding high on technology what was needed was building human capital of any organisation first. When she took over as the CMD in 2000, her predecessor was behind bars and the bank was on verge of closure, therefore she thought that the first aim was to rebuild the confidence of employees by making them do things inhouse. The subsequent steps taken included: 1. involvement of each and every employee of the organisation in the growth process by signing every staff with a crucial role, 2. Clear and transparent communication, 3. Identifying the strengths of the staff and by not critisising and discussing the failures of the past, 4. Imbibing a sense of righteousness in employees; and 5. Bosses stepping out of their God-like persona and agree to listen to employees who against bosses decisions.

Endnotes

On Mission Statements and Goal

1. **Ralph Waldo Emerson:** The world makes way for the man, who knows where he is going.
2. **D.S. Hunt:** Goals are dreams with deadlines.
3. **David Joseph Schwartz:** Think little goals and expect little achievement. Think big goals and win big success.
4. **G. Narayana:** Actions arising from clarity lead to efficiency and effectiveness.....clarity gives peace of mind and peace enhances the clarity. Peace of mind and clarity are the results of dedication and self-control of the responsible leader.
5. **Brian Tracy:** Goals are the fuel in the furnace of achievement.
6. **Abraham Lincoln:** A goal properly set is half way reached.

On Experiential Learning

1. **Swami Sukhabodhananda (2007):** To experience an experience is an art. We don't experience an experience, we always interpret an experience......To live wisely means to create a space in one's mind, which is capable of seeing and not just interpreting. Then one is available for experience.
2. **Eleanor Roosevelt:** People grow through experience if they meet the life honestly and courageously. This is how character is built.
3. **Bob Packwood,** American Politician: Good judgment comes from experience. Experience comes from bad judgment.
4. **Joseph Campbell,** American Mythologist and Writer: All you can learn is what your own inward life is and try to stay loyal to that.
5. **Epictetus,** Greek Philosopher: When you are offended at any one man's fault, turn to yourself and study your failures then you will forget your anger.
6. **E.E. Cummings,** American Poet: We do not believe in ourselves until someone reveals that deep inside us something is valuable,

worth listening to worthy of our trust, sacred to our touch.....that reveals the human spirit.

On Focal Person *Work Group Interactive Sessio*

1. **Socrates:** Think not those faithful who praise all thy words and actions, but those who kindly reprove thy faults.
2. **Martin Buber, Austrian,** Jewish Philosopher: Expounder of 'I-thou relation: Interconnectivity and Personal Identity'.
3. **Eugene T. Gendlin,** American Philosopher: Focusing, to connect with oneself, others.

Appendix: The 3-D process in action: *Spandan* workshops at Delta Information Services Limited, Chandigarh, India May 2007 – appended after Epilogue.

❑❑❑

9

Spandan 3-D Process:
Insights and Issues

Don't let the noise of other's opinions drown your own inner voice. And, have the courage to follow your heart and intuition. They somehow already know what you truly want to be come. Everything else is secondary.

– Steve Jobs

In the difficult times and challenging environment sometimes one feels like giving up and mind and heart shrink. With positive minds and persistent effort, one can always find life at the end of the tunnel. If your effort is more than the other people and your mind and heart is bigger, you can always overcome difficult times. It is extremely important to explore the alternatives and with purity of mind and not looking too much on some factors, one can always find truth and find a way. With innovative thinking and expanding one own mind and heart, one can conquer the world.

— S.H. Konosuke, Matsushita

It may be recalled that the 3-D Process of *Spandan* for inculcating values in work situations originated from the felt need of the participating organisations in the AICTE Emeritus Fellowship Study of Self Control as a Managerial Value (2001). Twelve industrial organisations and seven management institutions and the author started working upon and improvising on the 3-D process of Diagnosis, Discovery and Development of inculcation of values.

After the formation of ***Spandan*** in 2001, around a dozen organisations and institutions participated in short term workshops, varying between one and three days for acquainting themselves with the process. Five organisations, however, opted for undergoing at least one cycle of 3-D process requiring around an year depending upon the size and locations of the given organisation.

As a result, from time to time, issues have been accumulating, crystallizing and calling for attention and resolution by ***Spandan*** and the client organisations. Some such major issues are:

1. Awareness unaccompanied by Action.
2. 'Optimal' balance between Results and Relations.
3. Possession, Projection and Perception of communication and behaviour.

9.1 Awareness Unaccompanied by Action

Values, or strong beliefs about what is good or not, play an important role in individual as well as collective action. The human being has had been striving endlessly to improve upon himself through continuous search of values which would enrich him as a good human being. In the process, he did succeed in identifying suitable human values. Such identification however was not always leading him to their implementation. If, for example, he knew that truthfulness was an important human value, he might not be always able to be truthful. This gap between the knowledge of what is good and the inability of doing the said good has had been repeating itself over and over again, This gap, or dilemma, can be denoted as Awareness accompanied by Action.

The study of Human Values in Industrial Organisations (G.P. Rao 1996), reveals tellingly the gap and dilemma of managers of Awareness accompanied by Action in industrial organisations in our country. The study had 396 respondents of whom 144 were managers from different industrial organisations of the country. The ranking given by these managers for the top 10 values which were desired and practised respectively in industrial organisations in India are as on page 79.

The table reveals, of the 10 values (out of a total of 44-Spectrum of Human Values) which were perceive as more desirable, only one, *i.e.*, Prosperity, was also perceived to be more practised. Even this congruence between desirability and Practicability is to be seen, in the context that the other value in the Dyad, namely happiness is conspicuous by its absence. This would mean that it is not the Happiness, which is psychic in the nature, which is not sought after but Prosperity, which is materialistic in nature, which is given greater importance in work situations today.

Secondly, of the remaining nine values, four values namely, Fairness, Human Beings, Results and Community Interest, did not figure in the top 10 values perceived as being more practised. As can be noted, these four values are essentially humanistic. In their place we find Controlling Others, Material Comforts, Profits and Verifying before trusting others, were perceived as being

Table 9.1 Rankwise analysis of Desirable and Practised Human Values in Industrial Organsiation.

Top Ten Human Values Perceived as Desirable in Industrial Organisations	Concerned Value Dyad	Top Ten Human Values Perceived as More Practised in Industrial Organisations
Creativity	Conformity – Creativity	Controlling Others
Devotion to Duty	Devotion to Duty – One's own Need	Acquiring Resources
Professional Attachment	Emotional Detachment Professional Attachment	Material Comforts
Employee Development	Employee Performance Employee Development	Prosperity
Fairness	Fairness Firmness	Conformity
Human Beings	Human Beings Rules and Regulations	Customer Demand
Results	Relation Results	Profit
Sharing Resources	Acquiring Resources Sharing Resources	One's own Needs
Community Interest	Community Interest	Verifying before trusting others
Prosperity	Happiness Prosperity	Employee Performance

practised. These four values are essentially materialistic (Material Comforts and Profits) or inimical to other persons (Controlling Others and Verifying before trusting others). We thus find a situation that managers in India perceived essentially humanistic values were more desirable but ended up practicing in their place primarily Materialistic and inimical values,

Finally, the remaining five values perceived as more desirable but not as practised were: Creativity; Devotion to Duty; Employee Development; Sharing resources and Community Interest. These five values, again are humanistic (Employee Development; Sharing resources and Community Interest) or positive (Creativity and Devotion to Duty), In their place, the five values which were figuring were :Conformity, Ones own needs; Employee Performance; Acquiring Resources and customer Demand. It is significant – rather sad – that these two sets of values are inimical to each other. For example, Creativity and Conformity cannot go hand in hand. Also, four out of these five more practised values, are essentially individualistic (Acquiring Resources and Ones own needs) or non positive (Conformity and Employee performance).

The above empirical data on managerial perceptions thus indicate the lack of strong will and determination on the part of an elite group of persons, such as managers, in so far as:

- They fail to practice the human values, they consider desirable in their own organisations
- Those which were considered desirable, were essentially humanistic, whereas those which were practised were primarily individualistic and
- Such type of incongruence and contradictions in what was perceived desirable and practised otherwise to the extent of 50%

We thus come to a situation where a manager finds himself entrapped, in his inability or unwillingness in doing what he thinks as right. The dilemma of Awareness Unaccompanied by Action thus unfortunately stands confirmed.

That was what, perhaps Bengt Gustavsson meant, when he said, "We have enough of hypocrites, who are saying one thing and doing another".

9.2 'Optimal' Balance between Results and Relations

Human values are meant to aid the management in improving the performance of the organisation. Therefore, the selection of value should be such that the mission statement of the organisation is accomplished as effectively as possible. The mission statement can be accomplished affectively when the task function and social – emotional function are attended to equally. The task at hand should be accomplished; and at the same time, the morale of the employees should be kept high. What is needed therefore is an optimal balance between Results and Relations.

The next issue is, how do we know as to whether the values selected by an organisation have obtained such optimal balance between Results and Relations. As discussed earlier certain values are organisation specific, with emphasis on tasks and results. Certain other values are individual specific and are social – emotional and emphasize on relations. There are certain other values which are common in the sense that they are equally organisation and employee oriented. The implication is that the value selected should have more of less equal number from each category.

As an illustration, let us refer to the minutes and proceedings of the Delta Information Services, Chandigarh appended at the end.

Round 13 of the workshop contains the relevant particulars. The eight members participating in the workshop selected eight values after going through their identification at individual, small group and the core group levels. The group then wanted to examine whether these values when adhered, would lead the organisation to have a good fit between Results and Relations.

The identified values and their categorization by the core group are shown below:

Value	Company	Customer	Employee	Stake Holders
Conviction			✓	
Creativity	✓		✓	
Competition			✓	
Discipline			✓	
Devotion to duty			✓	
Employee Performance (present)	✓		✓	
Commitment			✓	
Profits	✓			✓
Customer Orientation		✓		

The deduction was that the mix isn't good enough as the major inclination is towards the 'employees', whereas it should be balanced. Hence, the Values may have to be re-visited.

Accordingly the core group continued the exercise in the next round.

Round 14 Task: Small Group; Focus: To identify 5 values from the Management cum Professional's point of view – Which 5 values if made part of work ethics, will motivate you to give the best to the company?

The values finally identified were:

- Employee needs
- Customer orientation
- Conviction
- Prosperity
- Creativity

The issue of optimal balance between Results and Relations incidentally addresses the question raised by Bengt Gustavsson as to how to distinguish values suitable for their orientation in work situations from the total array of values.

9.3 Possession, Projection and Perception of Communication and Behaviour

Values, unlike knowledge and skills cannot be taught or imparted. These are to be believed in at conscious level (*MANASA*), projected properly through the communication (*VACHA)* and conduct (*KARMA*). The expected outcome is that the others perceive and believe what is projected. Values in other words should become anchors for one's way of life. Also they are to be propagated and inculcated to fit in our thinking at individual, institutional and societal levels. It was Bertrand Russell, the noted British Philosopher, who said: "Without civic morality communities perish; without personal morality their survival has no value".

Two observations may be made at this point. The first is that while trying to understand and develop the necessary skills for possession and projection, the participants were finding it extremely difficult, particularly with reference to the corresponding perception by others. A person, who strongly believes in a value – let us say Fairness- and tries to project through his communication and conduct may not be perceived by others as a person of fairness.

As an aid to develop the skills for having congruent possession, projection and perception, a mechanism has been developed, christened as 'Focal Person – Work Group Interactive Sessions' as an integral part of the 3-D process.

The mechanism involves that each person of the core group assumes the role of focal person on the basis of rotation. He will interact with his work group members or team, to understand his areas of strength and areas for improvement so that he can become more effective in his performance. Experiential learning is used for the purpose which consists of introspection by the focal person and the feedback by the work group members. The incident method is found to be extremely effective for having greater focus and depth in the discussions and deliberations.

The second observation relates to the set of implications and insights one could discern from these three P's. Implications are far reaching. An honest person may be perceived as dishonest. A dishonest person may be perceived as honest. This will however be a short term phenomenon. The real worth or 'the true colours', as the case may be are bound to be noticed sooner than later. A sustaining congruence between and among possession, projection and perception will take place only when the person concerned has conviction in the values espoused by him. Conviction, as is known' is the willingness and ability of a person to 'burn himself' for the cause he believes in. This issue, incidentally, is reinforcing the statement of Bengt Gustavsson to the effect that value adherence should go beyond "intellectual embracement of concepts and are to be inculcated in the emotions, body and flesh of the manager and his organisation."

The other insight, as a corollary, is that of the importance of perception of a person in understanding and assessing the other person. What he perceives as the quality of the other person becomes a reality and fact for him – independent of whether it is the reality and fact or not. More often than not, he does not have the time, inclination or capability to verify before coming to a conclusion and forming an opinion about the person. This is very much so, when the opinion is negative about the other person. Again, the chances are that such an opinion is negative- because of the syndrome "I am OK – You are not OK" That is why it is said that wars start in the minds of people. We are afraid of our own shadows. The history of mankind bears testimony to this.

The implications of these two insights- one could think of many more- for management are two-fold: First, make sure that you are free, or make sure that you become free from such an human inclination and weakness. Later, enable others to cope with this human tendency. You have, in other words, to become subject and object for bringing about change in the self; and, become the subject, the catalyst, for bringing about change in others, who will be the objects in the processes of change at individual and institutional levels. This, as can be recalled, is the basic premise and thrust of this work: Emphasis: on self. Let us remake ourselves, by rekindling the innate divinity in ourselves. This is in fact the basic and the only thrust and the quest of mankind: How to reinvent ourselves as human beings!

❑❑❑

PART III

A Point of View:
Transformation through Human Values

The human behaviour operates at three planes. These are mental (*manasa*), verbal (*vacha*) and conduct (*karmana*). The components integrating these three planes of human behaviour are Knowledge, Skills and Attitudes. Knowledge refers to awareness, cognition. Skills relate to action, conation. Attitude refers to predisposition of mind, emotional. These three components in other words address the issues of what, how and why of human behaviour respectively.

Human values are considered as strongly held positive attitudes. The relationship between attitude and values and its relevance to the transformation process thus become the focus of the first chapter in this Part (**Chapter 10**). The next chapter (**Chapter 11**) postulates that such transformation gets institutionalized when it becomes part of management philosophy and institution building. **Chapters 12 to 14** discuss the transformation of management of self at individual, professional and organisational levels respectively. Instruments developed by the authorities concerned are used as the studies of reference for the analysis. The inputs emanating from these three chapters are compared with the Spectrum of Human Values in Industrial Organisations developed by G.P. Rao. This spectrum of human values is used as the instrument for inculcation of human values in an organisation by Spandan (**Chapter 15**). The last chapter, **Chapter 16**, aims at understanding the role of Community Service as a human value in management philosophy and institution building. Jaipur Rugs Company Pvt. Ltd., Jaipur, India, has been taken as a case study for the purpose.

10

On Attitudes, Human Values and Transformation

If we could see the miracle of a single flower clearly, our whole life would change.

— Lord Gautam Buddha

Your attitude, not aptitude, determines your altitude.

— Zig Zigler

10.1 On Attitudes

10.1.1 A Determinant and A Deterrent

If one is to pick up any letters in the English alphabets (*a*) which should have meaning of their own, two alphabets A and I qualify; and (*b*) which should have played an important role in human history, one is likely to choose – rightly at that, the letter 'I'.

'I' stands for ego in Latin and '*aham*' in Sanskrit. It would not be difficult to see the importance of the concept of 'I' in the human history and its progress. But for the desire on the part of individuals to do something more, different and better, the progress of mankind would not have been as it is today.

A little reflection, however, would also indicate the other side of the picture, .namely the undesirable consequences of either too much or too little of 'I'. The widely known saying that 'wars start in the minds of people' is but an example of how an hurt ego – genuine or otherwise – can become the source of misery to self and to others. The present day sociological problems like apathy and anomie are on the other hand the illustrations of too little involvement of an individual in men and matters.

The concept of 'I' applies with greater relevance and force to management. The reasons are manifold:

- The manager is a scarce resource
- He comes from those strata in the society which are even today strong socially, economically and politically
- The manager is placed in a position from where he can influence for good or bad, the destinies of others

The overall result is a high degree of self-image and adulation reciprocated by *prima facie* equally high degree of adulation from others. Another overall result of equal importance is low image of others. Two illustrations may be offered to bring home the managerial tendency of overestimating self and underestimating others.

The first illustration is a research study conducted by K.M. Thyagarajan (19103) in five companies in Tamil Nadu, involving 109 managers and 232 workers as respondents. The study was designed to reveal the extent to which managers and workers in India perceive each other's value system accurately. While the perception of both, the managers and the workers was by and large favourable towards self, this tendency was more marked with the managers. On a very positive dimensions, the managers estimated themselves higher than that for workers. On the dimension of work ('to work hard') for instance managers estimated themselves at 4.1 (out of a maximum of 5) as against 3.18. The workers, on their part, estimated on the same dimension of work, themselves at 3.810, a against 3.93 for managers – their by giving due credit to managers.

The second illustration refers to the experience the author have had since early seventies as a researcher and consultant in management. The sensitivity training offered to an estimated 5000 trainees in the country – spanning the period consisted of top and senior professionals in management and administration, academia, education administrators, prospective professional, trade union leaders, social service organisations and top and senior functionaries from the Army, Navy, and Airforce. Invariably almost always, the self assessment used to come highest and higher than of others. This tendency was found to exist even between the highest level in the corporate structure. Perceptual gap was found between the heads of the departments and their immediate subordinates. Further, the heads of the departments thought that an important need of their immediate subordinate was money. On the other hand, subordinates felt that it was greater autonomy and appreciation that they were looking for from their superiors.

10.1.2 Self-Discovery

Referring to people and their knowledge of men and matters, an Arabian proverb says that there are four sorts of men:

- He who knows not and knows not he knows not; he is a fool, shun him.
- He who knows not and knows he knows not: he is simple, teach him.
- He who knows and knows not he knows: he is asleep, wake him.
- He who knows and knows he knows: he is wise, follow him.

The proverb can be paraphrased in the form of a paradigm as follows:

	Knows Not	Knows
Knows Not	Fool (Shun)	Simple (Teach)
Knows	Asleep (Awake)	Wise (Follow)

When we look at the proverb a little deeper, with reference to the knowledge of self, however, several questions crop up. One set of them would judge us on the extent of our knowledge. Is it that we do not know about ourselves, but think that we know all of ourselves? Or we know all of ourselves but think that we know part of ourself only? The answers can be Yes to both these questions, primarily because of our perception being subjective and selective and our state of consciousness being predominantly sub subconscious and unconscious.

The other set of queries would be about the desire of a person to know: do we want to know about ourselves. The answer perhaps is yes, if the others perception is favorable to us. Do we still want to know about ourselves when the others perception relates to our areas of weakness and failure and therefore could be negative. The answer is both, yes and know. Yes, at intellectual level: we would like to know our weaknesses, because only then we can improve upon ourselves. No, at emotional level: while we are interested in knowing our weaknesses, we think others do not know them and hence are surprised. This surprise may be followed by three possible emotional states:

Elation: When a person close to us but about whose maturity we are not aware (for *e.g.*, daughter, son, student, sub-ordinate).

Hurt: When a person is close and liked but feedback is perceived to be given in an inappropriate time and place.

Anger: When a the feedback comes from a person about whom we do not have positive image and when we feel feedback is perceived to be given by the person at an appropriate time and place.

Rage: Enraged when the feedback comes from an individual about whom we do not have positive image and when we feel feedback has been given by the person at an inappropriate time and place.

(Base: Rao, G.P., An Odyssey to Self-Discovery, The Hindu, May 5, 1998)

10.1.3 Self-Discovery and Experiential Learning – A Way Out

Self-discovery is necessary for one's improvement of self. It is necessary because it gives an opportunity to look into oneself through introspection. Self-discovery through introspection is necessary but not sufficient, because the others perception is not included. Feedback therefore becomes an important component in self discovery. Introspection and feedback constitute experiential learning.

Experiential learning has been found to be very effective in dyad relationships, family, and friendships. It has also been found effective in work groups and organisational context. Experiential learning has been made an integral part in the 3-D process of Diagnosis, Discovery and Development of Spandan.

10.2 On Human Values

Like most areas of human knowledge and experience, the concept of human values defies definition. "Yet", as stated by Bengt Gustavsson *et al.*, "it can be instinctively felt, cognitively grasped, discussed as a shareable experience, and thus made a valid area of enquiry." (B. Gustavsson, A.N. Tripathi and G.P. Rao, Teaching Managers Human Values, Mimeo, 1996.) This enquiry is a major under current of the wisdom of literature of all the ancient civilization and of the later day philosophers, scholars and great leaders of social and political movements.

10.2.1 Classification of Human Values

The phenomenon of human values can be classified in two respects:

- In terms of approaches;
- In terms of the level of aggregation.

■ Approaches to Human Values

A perusal of available literature and sources indicates that the approaches to human values can be classified into two broad categories: Ideal – Normative; and, Empirical – Purposive.

Let us now try to understand the meanings of these approaches:

Ideal – Normative

S.K. Chakraborty, a pioneer in human values in management education in India, and belonging to the Ideal Normative category, defines a human value as "the manner in which an individual tends to make judgments or choices both about goals and means at different stages of one's life, in different facets of it , as are deemed to lead to the well being and happiness of oneself and society." (1990.)

In the Western tradition, Ideal normative approach is represented by Plato's formulation of the absolute values of truth, Goodness and Beauty. In the Indian tradition, absolute values are related to absolute reality whose nature is described as *Sat, Chit* and *Anand* Attainment of a state of eternal bliss by the realization of identity of the individual self with the universal self of this absolute reality is the highest object of human striving. The Ideal-normative approach has two subgroups:

- The first is the theistic view. It is based on a metaphysical belief system which accepts the reality of a divine cosmic order and faith in the authority of a creator God who is also the upholder of all values.

  Many leaders of the Indian renaissance like Swami Vivekananda, Sri Aurobindo, Rabindranath Tagore and Mahatma Gandhi used the view for their efforts at the spiritual, social and political rejuvenation of the Indian society. Academicians like S.K. Chakraborty (Human Values for Managers, Wheeler, 1995; and, Ethics in Management, Oxford University Press, 1995) and thinkers like Swami Ranganathanand (Human Values in Management, Bharatiya Vidya Bhavan, 1991) have used this theistic approach to value system.

- The second sub group can be called as Humanistic approach containing the ideas of humanists having varying degrees of theistic, non-theistic and atheistic leanings but attaching prime importance to man and human values. These ideas range from love and compassion of Lord Buddha to the radical humanism of Karl Marx The term human values has generally been understood in this context of humanistic thoughts. The present work for example, rests on this viewpoint.

Empirical – Purposive

The second main approach to human values can be categorized as Empirical-Purposive adopted by modern psychologists and other social scientists like Milton Rokeach. He defines "A value as an enduring belief that a specific mode of conduct or end-state of existence is personally or socially preferred to an opposite or converse mode of conduct or end-states of existence along a continuum of relative importance." (The Nature of Human Values, Free Press, (19103).

■ Human Values by Aggregation

Another way of understanding the phenomenon of human values is in terms of the level of aggregation they focus their attention on. These levels may broadly be Individual, Sociological and Ecological When focused at an individual as an independent entity, certain values which become relevant are survival, character, human rights and self realization. At the second , sociological level, values associated with family and other social institutions and professions become important .Finally, at the ecological level, human values focus on the interdependency of human beings and nature and include respect and harmony with nature, concept of Mother Earth, Sustainability and Eco Literacy.

We thus arrive at a two- dimensional matrix for the classification of human values. One dimension of this matrix consists of the three approaches; and, the other of the three levels of aggregation These two dimensions are represented below through horizontal and vertical columns respectively:

Table: Two Dimensional Classification Framework of Human Values

Approach / Level	Ideal – Normative		Empirical Purposive
	Theistic	Humanistic	
Individual	*	*	*
Sociological		*	*
Ecological			*

Understandably, the above classifications are by no means mutually exclusive and do not represent watertight compartments For instance, many of the humanistic approaches have theistic foundations. Similarly many items of the empirical approach are reformulations of the idealistic approach.

It is however significant that the progression in the above matrix, both in the horizontal and vertical directions, represents a chronological order. The earliest human value perceptions were related to the individual level. The growing complexities and tensions of the human societies enlarged the scope to include the sociological considerations in the second focus; and, the ecological concerns in the third.

10.2.2 CORE HUMAN VALUES

Averroism is a school of philosophy founded by Ibu Rushd Averroes (1126-1198), a Muslim philosopher, physician and master of Theology. Averroism, believes that religion and philosophy are different ways of reaching the same truth. One of its main ideas is that all humans at the basic level share the same divine soul.

Human being is thus divine and has the innate desire to be of help to others. This indicates that he is essentially normative in the approach. As has been accepted what distinguishes a human being from others is the ability to distinguish good from bad. The orientation of values accordingly is inbuilt in human personality.

Love and Compassion, Trust and Peace have been considered universal values aimed at enabling human beings elevate themselves from the lower self (i) to Higher Self (I). Gautama Buddha, for instance, preached: "Teach this triple truth to all: A generous heart, kind speech and a life of service and compassion are the things which renew humanity."

10.2.3 Core Values at Individual Professional, Organisational, Societal and Universal Levels

As transformational agent, a manager has to target for (*a*) change of attitudes, (*b*) by identifying suitable strongly held positive attitudes, *i.e.*, values and (*c*) propagating and inculcating these values, so that (*d*) the desired objective of rekindling the innate divinity is achieved in (*e*) the expected manner and form at (*f*) individual, professional and organisational levels.

Targeting for change of attitudes at each of the three levels, *viz.*, individual, professional and organisational, the manager should assume the role first as the object and later as the subject. That means he should go through the transformation himself before trying to transform others at any or all of these levels.

For identifying suitable select values at individual, professional, organisational, societal and universal levels, the values emanating from the following five studies were considered as the initiators:

1. Endorsement of values or standards of importance as the foundation of the ethics of Organisation Development (OD) – Human Systems Development (HSD) on an annual basis since 1990 (William Gellerman 1990).
2. Values emanating from the studies of Buddhism, Vedantas and yogic psychology as well as derivative epic and *Pauranic* literature and rooted in the deep structure of Indian culture and society as developed by S.K. Chakraborty (1990).
3. Human Values discussed and developed by G.P. Rao, A.N. Tripathi and

David Andrews, Visiting Fellows at the Management Centre for Human Values (MCHV, Indian Institute of Management, Calcutta (IIMC)), 1995.

4. Human Values in industrial organisations: a spectrum developed by G.P. Rao as result of six phase research: Review of Literature; Pilot study; Preliminary finalization (value dyads); field work; expert opinion; and finalization (1996) and

5. Key core values of global leaders emanating from global leadership survey (Ed Cohen, 2007)

The values emanating from the above studies are enclosed as Endnotes of this chapter.

The values at different levels were collated emerging from the above studies and used as anchors for humanising management at the respective levels. The next three chapters, Chapters 12-15, take the values developed by G.P. Rao *et al.*, Ed. Cohen and OD-HSD as studies of reference for analyzing transformation of management of self at individual, professional and organisational levels respectively. The next chapter, Chapter 16, takes the Spectrum of Human Values developed by G.P. Rao as the study of reference for Spandan 3-D Process of Inculcation of human values in an organisation.

10.3 On Transformation

An anonymously authored bestseller, titled, "Vestiges of the Natural History of Creation", was published 15 years before the publication of Charles Darwin's 'On the Origin of the species by means of Natural Selection'. The book talks of 'Law of Development' in living creatures whereby 'one species transformed into another by external circumstances, in incremental stages, from simple life forms to complex lives'.

Darwin's theory of evolution was more specific, attributing the origin of species and their diversification to the manner in which the adapt themselves to the environment in order to survive.

Transformation involving adaptation of human being with their environment is thus an integral part of human growth and development. Human behaviour accordingly has been considered as a function of individual and self.

Swami Sukhbodananda (2008) envisages transformation of life in terms of opening up of different locks: lock of senses; the body lock; the emotional lock; intellectual lock and , the spiritual lock – in that order This incidentally fits into the Spandan approach of human personality of moving from 'i' (lower self) to 'I' (higher Self).

When applied to manager, "Transformation implies a process whereby an individual attempts to elevate his or her Consciousness (*Chetna)* so that various commonplace conflicts and dualities begin to be resolved/ reconciled at higher levels of synthesis." (S.K. Chakraborty, 1993). Chakraborty cites the following as examples of some of the dualities/conflicts pervading the Individual – Organisation interface: Personal goal vs. Organisational goal; Discipline vs. Autonomy; and, Doing vs. Becoming. With reference to the Organisation – Society interface, some such dualities/conflicts are: Change vs. Stability; Short term vs. Long term; and, Gross National Product vs. Gross National Character.

It is significant to note that the year 2009 has been designated as the 'Year of Change' by Japans' Chief Monk Seiban Mori at Kiyonizu Temple; or 'Kanji', the country's character in the year. The monk states that change is constant, which is nothing new. And adds that, however, 'it is the individual who must change'. This again synchronises with the believe of Spandan, that the critical factor in the transformation of human being is self.

10.4 On Attitudes, Values, Transformation and Leadership

The All India Management Association (AIMA), New Delhi commissioned the Foundation for Organisational Research (FORE) to conduct a study of the Indicators and Processes of Effective Management. A large number of professionals in business and industry (384) and the outside (129) but connected with management participated in the study as respondents.

Leadership was perceived as the first contributory factor for effective management; Employee feelings and sentiments as the first indicator of effective management; and, changes in Managerial attitudes and skills as the first change needed in the management (AIMA, 1984).

Such importance assumes greater significance when we realize that the greatest discovery of our generation is "that a human being can alter his life by altering his attitudes of mind." (William James). When we acknowledge that values are strongly held positive attitudes, we become aware of (*a*) the direction in which the managerial attitudes are to take place and (*b*) the importance of values as integral to such change process. Moving further, S.K. Chakraborty, the pioneer in orientation of human values in management education in the country, declares Managerial Transformation by Values as a Corporate Pilgrimage: "Values as a process- like transformation – are to be normative process. And since normative and the sacred go together, transformation by values can be characterized as a pilgrimage" (S.K. Chakraborty, 199). Finally, N.R. Naryana Murthy, the pioneer in inculcation of values in Indian industry,

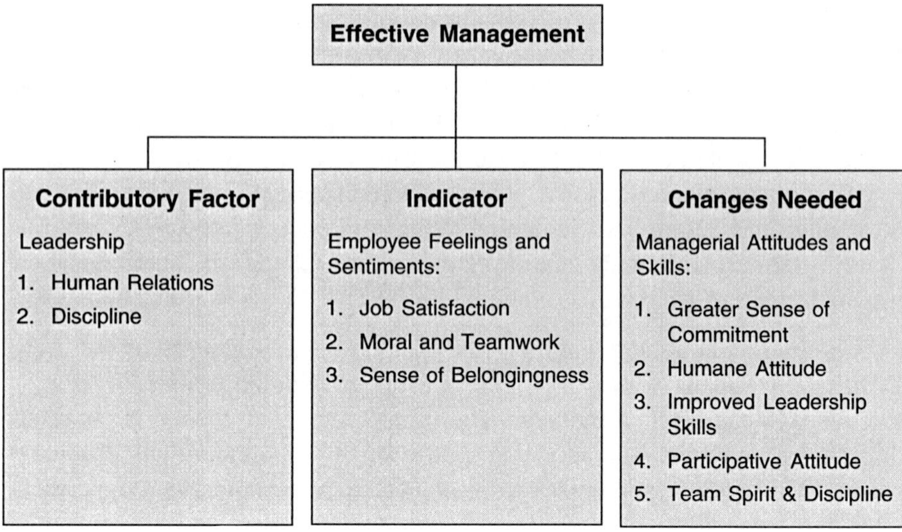

takes us to the ultimate in this process when he characterizes a leader as a transformational agent: "The primary role of a leader is to be a transformational agent because transformation is a big ticket progress. And progress is positive change. Progress is what is needed to make life better for any community, any institution. So the role of the leader is to marshal the resources required to achieve that transformation.... So the responsibility of a leader is to convert plausibly impossible targets into convincingly possible one." (N.R. Narayana Murthy, 2008).

Endnotes

1. Endorsement of values or standards of importance as the foundation of the ethics of Organisation Development (OD) – Human Systems Development (HSD) on an annual basis since 1990 (William Gellerman, 1990).

1. *Fundamental Values*
   - (*a*) Life and the quest for happiness
   - (*b*) Freedom, Responsibility and Self-control
   - (*c*) Justice
2. *Personal and Interpersonal Values*
   - (*a*) Human Potential and Empowerment
   - (*b*) Respect, Dignity, Integrity, Worth; and fundamental rights of individuals and other human systems
   - (*c*) Authenticity, Congruence, Honesty and Openness, Understanding and Acceptance
   - (*d*) Flexibility, Change and Proaction
3. *System Values*
   - (*a*) Learning, Development, Growth and Transformation
   - (*b*) Whole – Win Attitudes, Co-operation – Collaboration, Trust, Community & Diversity
   - (*c*) Widespread, meaningful participation in system affairs, democracy; and appropriate decision making
   - (*d*) Effectiveness, efficiency and alignment

2. Values emanating from the studies of Buddhism, Vedantas and yogic psychology as well as derivative epic and Pauranic literature and rooted in the deep structure of Indian culture and society as developed by S.K. Chakraborty (1990).

1. The individual must be respected
2. Co-operation and Trust
3. Jealousy is harmful for mental health
4. *Chitta-Shuddhi* or Purification of the mind
5. Top Quality Product/Service
6. Work is worship

7. Containment of Greed
8. Ethico-moral Soundness
9. Self-discipline and self-restraint
10. Customer Satisfaction
11. Creativity
12. The inspiration to give
13. Renunciation and Detachment

3. Human Values discussed and developed by G.P. Rao, A.N. Tripathi and David Andrews, Visiting Fellows at the Management Centre for Human Values (MCHV, Indian Institute of Management, Calcutta (IIMC)), 1995.

As part of the research work on Human Values in Management at Management Centre for Human Values (MCHV), Indian Institute of Management, Calcutta (IIMC), three of us Visiting Fellows at the MCHV, David Andrews, Australia, A.N. Tripathi, India and G.P. Rao, India) discussed several days to identify human values which could be considered as Core values desirable for mankind as a whole. Fifty such values classified under 18 clusters emerged, as below:

■ List of Fifty Human Values

1. Love, Affection, Concern, Kindness, Compassion
2. Courage, Conviction, Firmness, Perseverance
3. Gentleness, Courtesy, Sweetness
4. Honesty, Transparency, Credibility, Trustworthiness, Truthfulness
5. Friendliness, Supportive, Helpful, Cooperative
6. Creativity, Innovativeness
7. Open-Minded, Positive Attitude, Empathy
8. Patience, Tolerance, Forbearance, Self-Sacrifice
9. Tactfulness, Adaptability, Flexibility, Accommodativeness
10. Wisdom, Inquisitiveness
11. Self Restraint
12. Detachment
13. Respect for Nature and Dignity of Man
14. Humility, Modesty

15. Simplicity, Childlikeness
16. Industriousness, Material and Spiritual Self-Improvement
17. Sustainability, Frugality
18. Happiness, Enjoyment, Pleasure

4. Human Values in industrial organisations: a spectrum developed by G.P. Rao as result of six phase research: Review of Literature; Pilot study; Preliminary finalization (value dyads); field work; expert opinion; and finalization (1996).

1. Acquiring resources
2. Sharing Resources
3. Assertiveness
4. Support
5. Community Interest
6. Customer Demand
7. Controlling Others
8. Self-Control
9. Conviction
10. Compassion
11. Conformity
12. Creativity
13. Cooperation
14. Competition
15. Democracy
16. Discipline
17. Devotion to Duty
18. One's own Needs
19. Emotional Detachment towards enjoying benefits of results
20. Professional Attachment towards achieving results
21. Employee Performance (Present)
22. Employee Development (Future)
23. Fairness
24. Firmness
25. Freedom
26. Self-restraint
27. Happiness
28. Prosperity
29. Human Beings
30. Rules and Regulations
31. Material Comforts
32. Spiritual Pursuits
33. Profits
34. Service
35. Relations
36. Results
37. Shareholder's Claims
38. Employee Needs
39. Trusting Others
40. Verifying before Trusting others
41. Living for Work
42. Work for Living
43. *Quid pro quo (something done in return)*
44. Commitment

5. Key core values of global leaders emanating from global leadership survey (Ed Cohen, 2007).

1. Conviction
2. Diversity
3. Entreprenurship
4. Excellence
5. Fairness
6. Humility
7. Integrity
8. Passion
9. Perseverance
10. Positive Attitude
11. Respect
12. Service Oriented
13. Teamwork
14. Work-Life Balance

❑❑❑

11

Management Philosophy and Institution Building

Prerequisites of her Management Philosophy: Faith and Sincerity.
Approach: Consciousness.
Tool: Harmony. In thoughts and actions within and with others.
Aim: Perfection.

— **Mother's Ministry of Management, Pondicherry**

11.1 Management Philosophy: Indian Perspective (Base: Rao, G.P., 1992)

Management is defined as 'getting things done'. A Manager, accordingly, is expected to get desired results from and through people. For the purpose, he is expected to motivate, that is, 'induce' others such that they behave in the manner in which he wants them to behave. The focus of attention of management and manager is thus on results. While it is true that management and manager are to be result oriented, it appears that almost exclusive attention is laid on results and results alone. The management education and training, for example, talk of *Management by Results*. Several techniques and methods are being tried to enable the manager attain the results without fail. This almost exclusive attention on results, however, has led to certain undesirable consequences.

The manager's attempts on results has made him almost blind about the other aspects of task performance like human relations, sentiments, concern for others, etc.

Secondly, in his pursuit for getting results, a manager is likely to ignore, or sacrifice knowingly or unknowingly, the means adopted in achieving the said results.

Thirdly, the organisation's emphasis on measuring managerial performance through results has made the manager literally obsessed with results – thereby ignoring the long term interests of the organisation.

Fourthly, when the desired results are achieved, the manager is likely to attribute in all sincerity, perhaps the success to himself alone, whereas the fact is that no managerial success can be entirely attributed to the manager alone. His subordinates, colleagues and superiors along with the organisation as a system play equally important role in the success of a manager.

Fifthly, when the desired results are not achieved, the manager is likely to attribute the failure in all sincerity again - to anything and everything except self, whereas the fact is that no management failure could be attributed to others only. The manager's own limitations, weaknesses and frailties also play an equally important role in his not being able to get the desired results.

Sixthly, the obsession of a manager with results accounts for several executive health problems like high blood pressure, heart attack, ulcers, insomnia, tension, etc. Significantly, the executive health problems will be there whether the executive succeeds in getting desired results or not; when the desired results are obtained because of exertion, strain, tension, stress, etc., when the results cannot be got, then in addition to the problems of stress, etc., as indicated earlier, the problems like dejection, frustration, insomnia, which are essentially related to the failure on the part of the persons in achieving the desired results.

A perusal of the above analysis of the consequences of rather exclusive emphasis on results is very real, and is germane with catastrophic results - unless the whole issue is re-examined in its entirety. The very first question in such re-examination is to understand the expert to which a manager can assume responsibility for achieving the results. The answer to this question can be attempted through the following very simple but profound formula:

$$B = f(i, s) \text{ where}$$

B is Behaviour, i is Individual and s is situation

The above formula states that Behaviour (B) is a function of individual (i) and situation (s). This means that both the individual concerned and the environment within which he operates account for the given Behaviour. When applied to a manager, it means that managerial success or otherwise depends to some extent on others and their contribution or the lack of it.

I may illustrate the above point through one or two examples. A senior executive in New Delhi in an industrial group was found highly successful, and was deputed to take charge of one of its units located in Calcutta. For some months, he and the unit functioned without any friction. Soon thereafter, however, the unit experienced the longest strike in its history which lasted for nearly a year and resulted in huge losses in production, profits, wages etc. This illustration shows that while the person was the same, his ability to get desired result was not the same.

The second example relates to another senior executive stationed in Calcutta who was found to be very effective. He was deputed by the organisation to one of its units in Bangalore to deal with the rather turbulent situation there. With all his experience and expertise, and the full support of the top management, he just could not deal with the turbulent situation in Bangalore successfully. This illustration again brings me the fact that the given situation has a significant role to play in determining the ability of a manager in achieving or not achieving the desired results.

The foregoing analysis thus underscores the limits of managerial efforts at getting the results. When this proposition is accepted, another basic question arises: When a manager is not the sole factor in getting the result, to what extent can he assume the responsibility for the same? To what extent this rather obsessive pursuit for results is to be permitted?

The above discussion and depiction of the managerial obsession with results and its undesirable consequences thus calls for newer insight and answers, I submit, lies in our own tradition and ethos. I am referring to the concepts of '*Karmayoga*' and '*Sthitha Pragnya*' as propounded in the *Bhagwat Gita*. As is known, '*Karmayoga*' calls for action with indifference to the achievement or otherwise of results, and '*Sthitha Pragnya*' denotes equanimity whether the results are achieved or not. When adopted to the management context, the concepts of '*Karmayoga*' and '*Sthitha Pragnya*' would ordain incessant action accompanied by a high degree of equanimity on the part of the manager. In other words, a manager should aim at professional commitment when it is action, and emotional detachment when it is results. The above management philosophy based on the touchstones of '*Karmagoya*' and '*Sthitha Pragnya*', I believe, is the only realistic approach because of our earlier understanding that any achievement, behaviour, or result-getting is an outcome of the interface of individual and his environment, and cannot be attributed solely to either. This approach is most suitable to Indian context because the concepts such as '*Karmayoga*', '*Sthitha Pragnya*' have become the parts of Indian psyche.

The differences in the present approach of laying exclusive emphasis on results and the proposed approach based on professional commitment and emotional detachment and their consequences are depicted in the Exhibit.

EXHIBIT: Management Philosophy: Comparative Analysis

Aspect	Existing Approach *(Almost Exclusive Emphasis on Results)*	Suggested, Indian Perspective *(Professional Commitment and Emotional Detachment)*
Manager's obsession with 'result-getting'	Neglect of human aspects	Due consideration to human relation
Manager's obsession to 'somehow' get the results	Ignoring sacrificing Means-their ethicality in particular	Due importance to means, a better balance between ends and means;
Organisation's almost exclusive emphasis on results as the index of performance appraisal	Ignoring/neglecting long term perspective of the organisation, in particular	Due importance to long perspective of the term organisation and its members
Manager being able to achieve the results	Attributing the success to the self, egotism, complacency	Greater balance in assessing one's own contribution
Manager failing in getting the results	Attributing the failure to others, passing the buck	Greater balance in assessing the other's limitations
Managers failure *vis-à-vis* his health	Executive health – an important causality	Lesser executive stress

When I discussed the above ideas with a group of young, intelligent and prospective executives, the spontaneous reaction was: "Yes, it is true that what you are saying is desirable. But the question is, to what extent it is practicable." Significantly, the above question itself contains the answer-that is, while the concept of '*Karmayoga*' and '*SthithaPragnya*' are desirable their application is difficult. When the desirability of something is accepted, its practicability should not however really be difficult. It would, in other words, mean that greater and greater efforts of self analysis and self evaluation are to be made by managers at internalising the knowledge, skills and attitudes of '*Karmayoga*' and '*Sthitha Pragnya*' and infusing it with their work situation.

There is another word of caution: The sense of equanimity and detachment when over emphasized, may result in inactivity, defeatism and fatalism-in that order. The manager, accordingly, is to be ever careful in seeing that the very thin line between emotional detachment and inaction, etc., is not obliterated.

11.2 Institution Building and Management Philosophy

Management Philosophy is defined as the identification or development of knowledge, practices and policies of increasing degrees of generality relating to effective human behaviour in the context of work situations. A typical institution building involves five basic phases: inception, initial growth, and consolidation, further growth/decline: and, modified consolidation demise. At each phase of institution building, management philosophy becomes relevant and functional, so that the institution which is being built undergoes specific and distinct changes in its functioning.

An analytical framework is offered incorporating and developing upon these ideas on institution building and management philosophy.

The first broad premise is that institution building as influenced by its and the corporate management philosophy operates within certain contexts (environment): international; national; extra institutional; and, intra institutional. These specific elements of each such context are stated in the box on Environment. Certain select aspects of management philosophy, as mentioned in the second box are social values; value systems of institution builder; management assumptions about self and other; and, its behavioral manifestations.

The issues related to the juxtaposition of management philosophy and institution building are divided (Box 3) into four specific aspects: phases of Institution Building; Predominant Element (s) of Management philosophy; Interface; and Output (*vis a vis* Institution)

The first phase in the institution building is that of inception where the predominant element of management philosophy would be vision and conviction on the part of the institution builder(s). The said vision and conviction results in an infant vibrant institution coming into being through creation seizing of the opportunity in the environment.

The second phase in the institution building is the initial growth, wherein a high degree of commitment and competence from the institution builder (s) is required so that the newly born institution is inculcated with dynamism, as a result of which the institution starts growing. After the initial growth, it is found that the organisation needs to consolidate its policies, programmers and activities, which mark the third phase in the institution building. The concerned institution at that point is at a level of plateau. The needed consolidation can be achieved by the institution builder(s) through emotional detachment, by developing an autonomous organisational culture so that the institution pauses for a while – before launching upon the next phase- *i.e.*, further growth.

Management Philosophy and Institution Building

Environment

International Scenario
- Global Developments
- Demonstration Effect
- International Networking

National Context
- National Objectives and Dilemmas

Extra Institutional Environment
- Educational
- Sociological
- Cultural
- Legal
- Political
- Economic

Inter Institutional Networking

Institutional setting (sub systems)
- Goals SS
- Technical SS
- Structural SS
- Psycho social SS
- Managerial SS

→

Management Philosophy

Social Values

Value systems of institution builder
- Conviction
- Character
- Commitment
- Competence

Management Assumptions
- About self
- About others

Behavioural Manifestations
- Professional
- Commitment
- Emotional
- Detachment

Organisational Culture

→

Institution Building

Phases of institution building	Predominant element(s) of management philosophy	Interface	Output (*vis-à-vis* institution)
I Inception	– Vision-conviction	Creating/seizing the opportunity	Infant/ vibrant
II Initial growth	– Commitment – Competence	Inculcating Dynamism	Growing
III Consolidation (plateau)	– Emotional detachment	developing organisational culture	Pausing
IV Further growth (expansion/ diversification/ decline)	Renewed conviction and professional commitment/vision/ emotional detachment	Planned change	Developing/ decelerating
V Modified consolidation/ demise	Emotional detachment	Adaptiveness / acceptance	Mature/extinct

The fourth phase of institution building, *i.e.*, further growth, can be in the form of expansion and or diversification and or decline. The required expansions and or diversification could be achieved through the management philosophy, characterized by renewed conviction and professional commitment vision emotional detachment. The instrument (interface) to bring about such expansion diversification is planned change, whereby the institution concerned develops further. If, therefore, the institution builders are not in a position to visualise and prepare themselves and the organisation for adapting itself to move ahead, the consequence would be its decline and deceleration. This phase therefore is the most critical phase in as much as the very existence or the demise of the concerned institution is signalled during this phase.

The next (fifth) phase is modified or improvised consolidation, or alternatively the demise of the organisation. The congruent management philosophy during this phase is emotional detachment; the functional interface with the environment is the adaptiveness or acceptance of the institution, The end result (output) is that the institution becomes a mature one and become ready for further onward movement; or, for being bushed out of the industry.

We will have further analysis and insights on Institution building in chapter 16.

❑❑❑

12

Transformation of Management of Self at Individual Level

> *We must be silent before we can listen. We must listen before we can prepare. We must prepare before we can serve. We must serve before we can lead.*
>
> — **William A. Ward**

As transformational agent, a manager has to target for (*a*) change of attitudes, (*b*) by identifying strongly held suitable positive attitudes, *i.e.*, values and (*c*) propagating and inculcating these values, so that (*d*) the desired objective of rekindling the innate divinity is achieved in (*e*) the expected manner and form at (*f*) individual, professional and organisational levels.

Targeting for change of attitudes at each of the three levels, *viz.*, individual, professional and organisational, the manager should assume the role first as the object and later as the subject. That means he should go through the transformation himself before trying to transform others at any or all of these levels.

It may be recalled that Chapter Ten on Attitudes, Human Values and on Transformation, contained among others the instruments of human values at individual, professional and organisational levels by respective authorities. The three chapters, Chapters 12-14, take the values developed by G.P. Rao *et al.*, Ed. Cohen and OD-HSD as studies of reference for analyzing transformation of management of self at individual, professional and organisational levels respectively. The chapter to follow, Chapter 16, takes the Spectrum of Human Values developed by G.P. Rao study of reference for Spandan 3-D Process of Inculcation of human values in an organisation.

Transformation of self at individual level as human being is the focus of the present chapter. The objective is to have balance between head, heart, and spirit; to be good, and do good; to become some thing more, some thing different, some thing better; to move from 'i' (lower self) to 'I' (higher Self).

12.1 Identifying Human Values at Individual Level

Following is a table that provides data emanating from the five studies, of which study #3 has been taken as the study of reference. This study, Fifty Human Values (G.P. Rao, *et al.*, relates to the three Visiting Fellows, including the author, at the Management Centre for Human Values (MCHV), IIM Calcutta, 1995-96 identifying important human values at individual level through discussion and debate spread over a few weeks. The scholars identified 50 human values at individual level divided into 18 clusters.

Table 12.1 Select Human Values at Individual Level

Value	1	2	3	4	5	Total
Love			✓			1
Affection			✓			1
Concern			✓			1
Kindness			✓			1
Compassion			✓	✓		2
Sub-Total						6
Courage			✓			1
Conviction			✓	✓	✓	3
Firmness			✓	✓		2
Perseverance			✓		✓	2
Sub-Total						8
Gentleness			✓			1
Courtesy			✓			1
Sweetness			✓			1
Sub-Total						3
Honesty	✓		✓			2
Transparency	✓		✓			2
Credibility			✓			1
Trustworthiness		✓	✓			2
Truthfulness			✓			1
Sub-Total						8

Value	1	2	3	4	5	Total
Friendliness			✓			1
Supportive			✓	✓		2
Helpful			✓			1
Co-operative	✓	✓	✓	✓		4
Sub-Total						8
Creativity		✓	✓	✓		3
Innovativeness			✓			1
Sub-Total						4
Open Minded			✓			1
Positive Attitude			✓			2
Empathy			✓			1
Sub-Total						4
Patience			✓			1
Tolerance			✓			1
Forbearance			✓			1
Self-Sacrifice			✓			1
Sub-Total						4
Tactfulness			✓			1
Adaptibility			✓			1
Flexibility	✓		✓			2
Accomodativeness			✓			1
Sub-Total						5
Wisdom			✓			1
Inquisitivness			✓			1
Sub-Total						2
Self Restraint		✓	✓	✓		3
Sub-Total						3
Detachment		✓	✓	✓		3
Sub-Total						3
Humility			✓		✓	2
Modesty			✓			1
Sub-Total						3
Simplicity			✓			1
Childlikeness			✓			1
Sub-Total						2

Value	1	2	3	4	5	Total
Industriousness			✓			1
Material & Spiritual Development			✓	✓		2
Sub-Total						3
Sustainability			✓			1
Frugality			✓			1
Sub-Total						2
Happiness	✓		✓	✓		3
Enjoyment			✓			1
Pleasure			✓			1
Sub-Total						5

1. Endorsement of values or standards of importance as the foundation of the ethics of Organisation Development (OD) – Human Systems Development (HSD) on an annual basis since 1990 (William Gellerman, 1990).
2. values emanating from the studies of Buddhism, Vedantas and yogic psychology as well as derivative epic and *Pauranic* literature and rooted in the deep structure of Indian culture and society as developed by S.K. Chakraborty (1990).
3. Human Values discussed and developed by G.P. Rao, A.N. Tripathi and David Andrews, Visiting Fellows at the Management Centre for Human Values (MCHV, Indian Institute of Management, Calcutta (IIMC)), 1995.
4. Human Values in industrial organisations: a spectrum developed by G.P. Rao as result of six phase research (1996) and
5. Key core values of global leaders emanating from global leadership survey (Ed. Cohen, 2007).

The above table brings out top values and the associated clusters as follows:

Table 12.2 Valuewise Ranking at Individual Level

Associated Cluster	Value	Total	Rank
Friendliness	Co-operative	4	I
Respect for nature and dignity of man	Respect for nature and dignity of man	4	I
Courage	Conviction	3	III
Creativity	Creativity	3	III
Self-Restraint	Self-Restraint	3	III
Detachment	Detachment	3	III
Happiness	Happiness	3	III

Co-operative and Respect for nature and dignity of man occupy the first rank with four studies out of the five identifying them as important values.

Co-operative spirit being a top value is in keeping with latest thinking and theory of origin of man (Chap.2). Respect for Nature and Dignity of Man, the other top value is congruent with the basic premise of this work of the innate divinity in human being. S.K. Chakraborty defines the relevant value, *the individual must be respected,* "not because of his or her individuality but because of the transcendent, the divine enshrined in him or her, whether good or bad, older or younger, rich or poor".

The cluster of Friendliness, includes co-operative and creativity with four and three tally points each. This implies that it is interpersonal relationships that play an important role in the group functioning in an organisation.

12.2 Attitudinal Change and Adherence to Select Human Values

Having selected the values significant for transformation at individual level as human being, the issue to be addressed is, how to go about making self adhere the select values.

Attitudes take time to be formed; and take at least equally same amount of time to get changed. A whole lot of theory on Management of Attitude of Change with Kurt Lewin as the pioneer, is aimed at understanding the sources of resistance for change and how to manage change.

What, however, we try to understand is a highly insightful response to the issue, why the implementation of human values in the individuals is difficult?, by a young student of management at the threshold of his studies. At the end of the session on the issue, the said student submitted the Fig. 12.1 as his answer to the question.

The student visualized that human values permeate the environment, the outer world, and that it is for the individual concerned to respond and avail the opportunity of imbibing the suitable values. He feels that the following two factors stand in the way;

1. Self-Esteem is so much saturated that the individual thinks that there is no need of adapting the other values, from the outer world; and,

2. Due to some unethical and improper character, there lies the lack of desired level of adaptability of human values.

We thus comeback to the simple and significant equation that Behaviour is a function of Individual and Situation [Behaviour = f (i, s)].

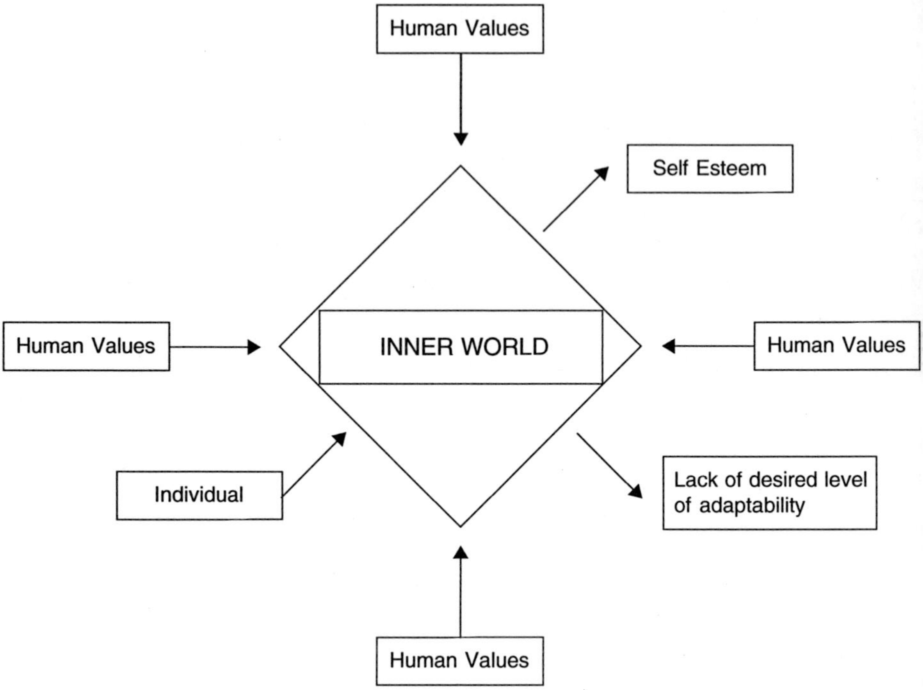

Fig. 12.1 "Why the implementation of Human Values in the individuals is difficult?:": The response of Harsh Awasthi, a student of management, 2005.

12.2.1 Attitudinal Change Agents

The attitudinal change and the accompanying process of inculcation of suitable values should therefore begin right at the infancy of the human being.

Family plays an important in the socializing process of the child with mother as the catalyst. As the Dalai Lama stated, "The parents will have to instill the values of love and contentment in the new generation. These are secular ethics, basic human values. For happiness in the future one has to take responsibility of his community… And this role can be best performed by the mother", by removing the element of sectarianism which might happen when the orientation of values is undertaken by religious or spiritual leaders. (The Dalai Lama: Messenger of Peace, *The Times of India*, January 1, 2001).

The role of Family and Mother in particular as socializing agent has been discussed at length as part of Maternalistic Management (Chapter 3). Analysis specific to the role of family value in management decision making is undertaken in Chapter 17.

The other important change agent is Education. The primary function of education is to transmit or pass on to the new generation a particular way of life (Orin Graff and Calvin M. Street, 1956). Relevant to the frame of reference of humanising people, a particular way of life which education can seek is how to humanise people. Value based education has had been developed and developing as a response.

When we look at the impact of education, however, the overall effect appears not to be satisfactory. As, for instance pointed out by Mahmood bin Muhammad, a former Indian diplomat, "The major aim of education is to humanize people. An efficient educator aims at enlightening the minds and illuminating the hearts of individuals. What is being done today is to educate the heads and hands and not the hearts. We rank third in the world in skilled manpower. The products of the present system are the better surgeons, better engineers and better scientists but, alas, not good human beings. They excel in science without conscience, politics without ethics, freedom without discipline and knowledge without wisdom" (Human Values, the missing link, *The Hindu*, November 26, 1996.).

The Dalai Lama, in a similar vein says, "Modern education does wonders for the brain, but does not develop the heart"

In view of the importance of education, the issue will be discussed in Chapter 17. (17.2)

The third change agent is Self. Who else is more interested and concerned about me than myself? Felt need is the therefore the first and crucial trigger for change. The next question is who will make me realize the need for change? The answer is, 'those who are interested in and concerned about me' 'Who are they, who are interested in and concerned about me?' 'Any body and everybody else- but most important is myself'. The buck stops at me. The buck keeps on coming back to me, again and again. The buck, as a matter of fact, has never left me, has always been with me and always will be with me.

How rich – and at the same time – how poor I am!

Endnotes

1. **K.M. Gupta,** The Ultimate Holy Book of Humanity in *The Times of India*, The best of Speaking Tree, Vol.2 2004: The ultimate ethic, the best possible ethic of the microcosm is harmony and concurrence with the ethic of the macrocosm. In being's especially human's the three metric properties – electricity, magnetism and gravitation – act as 'id', ego and super ego. By trying one's best to achieve the best possible balance of 'id', ego and super ego, and by leading them to the Unified Field through as much concentration and meditation as possible, one strikes the possible harmony and concurrence with the macrocosm – the ultimate ethic.

2. **Head and Heart, Albert Einstein:** The intuitive mind is a sacred gift and the rationale mind is a faithful servant. We have created a society that honors the servant and has forgotten the gift.

3. **William Hazlitt,** British Writer: The seat of knowledge is in the head, of wisdom in the heart.

4. **Carlos Castaneda:** Look at every path closely and deliberately, then ask ourselves this crucial question: Does this path have a heart?

5. **S.H. Konosuke, Matsushita:** In the difficult times and challenging environment sometimes one feels like giving up and mind and heart shrink. With positive minds and persistent effort, one can always find life at the end of the tunnel. If your effort is more than the other people and your mind and heart is bigger you can always overcome difficult times. It is extremely important to explore the alternatives and with purity of mind and not sticking too much on some factors, one can always find truth and find a way. With innovative thinking and expanding ones mind and heard one can conquer the world.

❑❑❑

13

Transformation of Management of Self at Professional Level

> *What is the purpose of life of a professional man? .... You have to go beyond your narrow professional boundaries, and with your special knowledge and skills, subserve broader social, and national purposes, unsullied by personal ambition and the need for wealth and recognition.*
>
> — Ravi J. Mathai

Transformation of management of Self at Professional level is the focus of the present chapter. The objective is to have balance between professional environment while working and emotional detachment about the outcomes of the work. To develop an equanimity as between; an attitude of *Karmayogi.*

13.1 Manager as a Professional: 'From Pirate to Prophet'

Friedrich Nietzsche, the celebrated German philosopher stated 'a la Nietzsche' that at one point of time, merchants and pirates were considered the same. The economic history, industrialisation process and the development of management thought and profession world over after the industrial revolution witnessed changes in the roles of the person who creates and manages in myriad manners. Merchant, trader, businessman, capitalist, industrialist, entrepreneur, institution builder, visionary and prophet have had been the *avataars* of the person who had been instrumental in creating, developing and destroying the destiny's of the countries in economic and financial terms.

In Indian context, (Chapter 5), the communities entrusted with the task of dealing with money (*Vaishya's*) under the caste system, played the pioneering role in industrialising the country. Managing agency system was the earliest form which came into vogue.

Subsequently, certain regions also having the elements of caste contributed in the process. These included *Marwaris* (originating from Rajasthan), *Gujaratis, Parsis* and *Chettiars* from the south.

In the later phase, with the introduction of education systems by Britishers in the country, people belonging to other communities and regions started joining factories, mines and plantations. Relatively, however, only a smaller proportion of them could reach the levels of management. After independence, several significant steps were taken by the government to accelerate the pace of industrial development of the country. These included, Industrial Policy Resolutions 1948 and 1956; Five Year Economic Plan; Socialistic pattern of society, declaration of the policy on Management education; culminating in privatisation, liberlisation and globalisation in 1991.

The cumulative effect of all these developments have been (*a*) increase in quantity and quality (to a lesser extent) of management as a resource; (*b*) marked shift from management class from Patrimonial to Professional and increased spheres of economic activity developing professional system of authority in their functioning.

13.2 Who is a Professional?

Like several concepts in management, Professional and Professionalism have attracted attention from academia and professionals, debated '*ad nauseam*', yet defying consensus on what they constitute.

The issues which need to be addressed in this respect include,

- What is Professionalism?
- What are its characteristics?
- Who is a Professional?
- What are his characteristics?
- How does a professional differ from a non and un-professional.

Confining to the distinguishing feature of manager as a professional, the basic issue is what is the mix of knowledge, skills and attitudes which should go into making a 'good enough' if not ideal professional? Is it the qualification (knowledge), experience (skills) and mindset (attitudes) which should be an important if not the only component. It is really difficult to answer this question. A person with qualifications may not turn out to be a good manager. A person without suitable qualifications may turn out to be a good manager. The utility of qualifications and knowledge is therefore zero to –ve. Similarly, a person with experience may or may not turn out to be a good manager. The impact of experience and skills is also indeterminate on the functioning of a manager. When not used properly, one's experiences thus become accumulations of follies and failures rather than becoming the triggers for better performance.

Compared to Knowledge and Skills, the role of attitudes appears to be rather obvious. One must have a appropriate mindset to be a successful manager. A suitable attitude thus becomes '*sine qua non*' for a professional and professionalism in management. Knowledge and skills become contributory factors to strengthening the managerial thinking, communication and action effectively.

13.3 Identification of Professional Values

Table 13.1 contains relevant data about the professional values of managers in the context of the globalization as emanating from the five studies under consideration. Out of these studies, Ed Cohen's ' Work Leadership without Borders; Successful strategies from World Class Leaders'(2007) has been taken as the study of frame of reference.

A global leadership survey was carried out on core values 'How You Are' of world class leaders based upon indepth interviews of eight such leaders. The survey resulted in the 14 core values as presented in Table 13.1.

Table 13.1 Select Human Values at Professional Values of Global Leaders

No.	Professional Values	1	2	3	4	5	Total
1.	Conviction			✓	✓	✓	3
2.	Diversity					✓	1
3.	Entrepreneurship					✓	1
4.	Excellence					✓	1
5.	Fairness	✓	✓		✓	✓	3
6.	Humility			✓		✓	2
7.	Integrity	✓				✓	2
8.	Passion					✓	2
9.	Perseverance			✓		✓	2
10.	Positive Attitude	✓		✓		✓	2

No.	Professional Values	1	2	3	4	5	Total
11.	Respect	✓	✓	✓	✓	✓	5
12.	Service Oriented		✓		✓	✓	3
13.	Teamwork	✓	✓			✓	3
14.	Worklife Balance					✓	1

1. Endorsement of values or standards of importance as the foundation of the ethics of Organisation Development (OD) – Human Systems Development (HSD) on an annual basis since 1990 (William Gellerman 1990).
2. values emanating from the studies of Buddhism, Vedantas and yogic psychology as well as derivative epic and *Pauranic* literature and rooted in the deep structure of Indian culture and society as developed by S.K. Chakraborty (1990).
3. Human Values discussed and developed by G.P. Rao, A.N. Tripathi and David Andrews, Visiting Fellows at the Management Centre for Human Values (MCHV, Indian Institute of Management, Calcutta (IIMC)), 1995.
4. Human Values in industrial organisations: a spectrum developed by G.P. Rao as result of six phase research (1996) and
5. Key core values of global leaders emanating from global leadership survey (Ed. Cohen, 2007)

From **Table 13.1,** one can find the top six values as presented below.

Top six professional values:

Table 13.2 Valuewise Ranking at Professional Level

Value	Total	Rank
Respect	5	I
Conviction	3	II
Fairness	3	II
Positive Attitude	3	II
Service Oriented	3	II
Teamwork	3	II

'Respect' has been identified as one of the important professional values in all the five studies. OD-HSD Values Study (No.1), describes 'Respect' along with 'Dignity', 'Integrity', 'Worth'; and 'Fundamental Rights' and other human systems as 'People appreciating one another and their rights as human beings including life , liberty and the quest for happiness.

The second study, S.K. Chakraborty (1991) states that the individual must be respected not because of his or her individuality but because of the transcendent, the divine enshrined in him or her, whether good or bad, older or younger, rich or poor'.

The concept of respect thus deepens with reference to the human being and widens to envelope other organic and inorganic systems apart from the human beings. At the ultimate, the respect assumes the theory of oneness where the entire cosmos is revered as Universal Consciousness.

13.4 Propagation and Inculcation of Professional Values

Individual and personal values start taking shape even before the birth of a human being. Called '*Sanskaras*', the values are the result of the individual and the environment of which he is a part. Professional values, on the other hand, assume importance later during the studentship period and more so at the time of assuming a career by the person. Unlike personal values, therefore, professional values cannot have universal appeal and application. They differ from professional to profession, country to country and time to time. Even then, it is possible and necessary to identify basic professional values which should be lodestars for a more meaningful and enriching professional lives. The professions encode such values in the form of professional ethics.

In India, professional ethics for managers is yet to be evolved. Subject to that, certain fundamental responsibilities of managers to their profession, the organisation, society/country and to themselves are to be delineated and encoded. The 14 key values emanating from the Global Leadership survey discussed above, may be used as a reference point.

The management education and industry have to work in tandem for the purpose of developing, implementing and enforcing values thus encoded. Equally important propagation and inculcation of those values through teaching, research, training and Facilitation (consultancy).

13.5 The Purpose of Life of a Profession: A Study of Perception by Management Students

This section aims at understanding the nature and extent of readiness and acceptance of the orientation of values in management profession by prospective professionals.

This study was conducted as part of teaching MBA, consisting of 26 students. The students were distributed the response of Ravi J. Mathai, an eminent management educationist and professional in the country, to the question, 'What is the purpose of life of a professional man?" The response of Mathai was as follows: "You have to go beyond your narrow professional boundaries, and with your special knowledge and skills, subserve broader social and national purposes, unsullied by personal ambition and the need for wealth and recognition." The students were to answer three questions;

1. To what extent – on a ten point scale – do you think that the above statement is realistic?
2. To what extent – on a ten point scale – do you think that the above purpose of life is being pursued by executives in Indian industry today?
3. To what extent – on a ten point scale – do you think you would be able to pursue the above purpose of life in your own career?

(G.P. Rao, 1985)

Table 13.3 Student responses

Question	Mean	Range	
		Minimum (n)	Maximum (n)
To what extent – **Realistic**	4.4	1 (1)	7(1)
Extent pursued by **Executives in India**	4.0	2 (2)	6 (5)
Extent to be pursued by **Self**	4.0	1(1)	7 (2)

Certain observations made by the students, explaining their response are insightful. To give an example of the response, "I am an ordinary man and not Vivekananda or Aurobindo to be without perosal ambition, desire for wealth and recognition. I do possess certain qualities which prevent me to work without personal ambition or fame and I feel that I am a perfect example for Marslow's Hierarchy model and only after satisfying my esteem needs, I can serve the society. I am not a Jesus Christ to serve the world knowing that one day or other I will be assassinated. But I have given myself four just because I have the inclination to serve and if given a chance I am ready to go beyond the narrow professional boundaries and subserve the broader, social and national purposes."

This is rather a sad commentary indeed, but perhaps reflects the society in which we are functioning. The other side of the picture, however is gratifying. The extent to which the statement was realistic was perceived at 4.4, which is higher than that of, the extent to which they themselves expect to follow in future (4.0). The gap between the perceived realism and perceived preparation by self is indicative of the room for improvement in their own perception and behaviour, since they are already convinced about the realism of the statement. In other words, they have to ignite themselves to be better professionals.

13.6 A Family Organisation at the threshold of Professionalism

The preceding section dealt with perceptions, expectations and apprehensions of a group of prospective professionals about their future career as professionals. This section offers a glimpse of a large public limited family organisation which is at the threshold of professionalism. The issue is reflected in the form of a letter written by the Joint Managing Director of the company to its Vice – Chairman, who is also his uncle. The excerpts from the letter are presented below.

1. **'Lack of Professionalism:** We have, almost always, worked with our gain in mind, an attitude more similar to the industry being our cow (by 'our' I mean our family). Because of this coloured vision we have tended to merge our family and proprietory interest into our sphere of work and thereby not being able to demand, expect and reward any fruitful contribution from our staff. On the surface of it, it may not appear to be of much significance; but on closer analysis, it would reveal that subconsciously we reflect a lack of trust in our own people and restrict very much their sphere of decision making (even clear upto the top level).

   This then results in our wasting too much of our time in day to day working decisions and obscure controls, while neglecting the much wider aspects of planning (both long and short range)...Incompetence in our staff is directly related to this. Competent staff will demand much free and congenial atmosphere than we can offer or have been offering.

2. Long range planning ability is obscured by immediate or very short term gains. Although it is very difficult to fix a time for short term gains, what I mean by this is that, we keep our system , product and even expansion or new ventures very rigid...

3. Perhaps the most important aspect of our failure has been a lack of creative leadership by us. True, by ourselves we may be very enthused about our work and even may think in terms of improvement also, but somehow or the other, we have not been able to communicate this spirit to our subordinates.

   We may say, whatsoever we may like about our sub ordinates, but it is a very important function of leadership to instill and excite the junior staff sufficiently to work with vigor and creativeness. We tend to create such aura of our object superiority amongst our staff that they fail to respond to our otherwise simple motivations. It is our responsibility to motivate them, guide them, remove fear of unforeseen mistakes and, above all, show ourselves to be able to respond to their ideas and be sensitive to their needs. We have to create atmosphere of job satisfaction in our sub ordinate staff – down to the lowest level. We must build our confidence in them to gain their confidence in us. It is a two way street, but we have to be the first and that also for a long long time. Above all, instead of an immediate performance result, that we demand now, we should be more than satisfied in gradual improvement and positive thinking. This alone, at a later stage, brings about much rapid improvements and that we have trying to achieve.

I hope that I have fairly, clearly expressed myself. These are strictly my own views and I will not be surprised if I am not widely off the mark. However, I do feel that there is some substance in what I have said."

❑❑❑

14

Transformation of Management of Self at Organisational Level

> *The organisational value most cherished, yet wanting, in India today is teamwork. The real answer to this gap is to develop the inner conviction and feel about one's true identity to be the Self and not self. Work from the plane of Self-perception will lead us to see unity in diversity.*
>
> — S.K. Chakraborty

The preceding two chapters offered important values suitable for transformation managers at individual and professional levels. We now look at important values expected to enable to the management as a group transforms themselves at organisational level.

14.1 Identifying Human Values for Management at Organisational Level

Table 14.1 contains relevant data about the organisational values for managers emanating from the five studies under consideration. The first study in this series refers to the values or 'standards of importance', annually endorsed by Organisational Development (OD) – Human Systems Development (HSD) as the foundation of their ethics. This study is used as the reference points.

Table 14.1 Select Human Values at Organisational Level

Value	1	2	3	4	5	Total
Fundamental Values						
1. Life and the Quest for Happiness	✓		✓	✓		3
2. Freedom, Responsibility & Self Control	✓	✓	✓	✓		4
3. Justice	✓			✓		3
Sub-Total						10
Personal and Interpersonal Values						
1. Human Potential and Empowerment	✓					1
2. Respect, Dignity, Integrity, Worth; Fundamental Rights of Individual and Other Human Systems	✓	✓	✓	✓	✓	5
3. Authenticity, Congruence, Honesty & Openness, Understanding & Acceptance	✓		✓		✓	3
4. Flexibility, Change and Pro-action	✓		✓			2
Sub-Total						11
System Values						
1. Learning, Development, Growth and Transformation	✓		✓	✓		3
2. Win – Win Attitude, Co-operation – Collaboration	✓	✓	✓	✓		4
3. Widespread Meaningful Participation in System Affairs, Democracy and Appropriate Decision Making	✓			✓		2
4. Effectiveness, Efficiency and Alignment	✓	✓		✓	✓	4
Sub-Total						13

1. Endorsement of values or standards of importance as the foundation of the ethics of Organisation Development (OD) – Human Systems Development (HSD) on an annual basis since 1990 (William Gellerman 1990).
2. values emanating from the studies of Buddhism, Vedantas and yogic psychology as well as derivative epic and *Pauranic* literature and rooted in the deep structure of Indian culture and society as developed by S.K. Chakraborty (1990).
3. Human Values discussed and developed by G.P. Rao, A.N. Tripathi and David Andrews, Visiting Fellows at the Management Centre for Human Values (MCHV, Indian Institute of Management, Calcutta (IIMC)), 1995.
4. Human Values in industrial organisations: a spectrum developed by G.P. Rao as result of six phase research (1996) and
5. Key core values of global leaders emanating from global leadership survey (Ed. Cohen, 2007)

Table 14.2 Valuewise Ranking at Organisation Level

Value	Total	Rank
Respect/Human beings	5	I
Self Control	4	II
Co-operation/Teamwork	4	II
Results/Industriousness/Excellence	4	II

14.2 Human Values at Individual, Professional and Organisational Levels: Summing Up

To do the above lets have a re-look at the valuewise ranking for each of the above.

Table 12.2 (Chapter 12) Valuewise Ranking at Individual Level

Associated Cluster	Value	Total	Ranks
Friendliness	Co-operative	4	I
Respect for nature and dignity of man	Respect for nature and dignity of man	4	I
Courage	Conviction	3	III
Creativity	Creativity	3	III
Self-Restraint	Self-Restraint	3	III
Detachment	Detachment	3	III
Happiness	Happiness	3	III

Table 13.2 (Chapter 13) Valuewise Ranking at Professional Level

Value	Total	Rank
Respect	5	I
Conviction	3	II
Fairness	3	II
Positive Attitude	3	II
Service Oriented	3	II
Teamwork	3	II

Table 14.2 Valuewise Ranking at Organisational Level

Value	Total	Rank
Respect/Human beings	5	I
Self-Control	4	II
Co-operation/Teamwork	4	II
Results/Industriousness/Excellence	4	II

Table 14.3 Valuewise Ranking: A birds eye view

Rank	Individual	Professional	Organisational	Weighted Values* (points)
I	Co-operative			2**
I	Respect/ Human beings	Respect	Human Beings	6
II	Conviction	Conviction		2
II	Creativity			1
II	Self-Restraint		Self-Control	2
II	Detachment			1
II	Happiness			1
	–	Fairness		1
	–	Positive Attitude		1
	–	Service Oriented		1
	–	Teamwork	Co-operation	2**
	–	–	Results/ Industriousness/ Excellence	1

* Weighted Values are computed by according two points for the first rank and one point for the second rank.

** Total weighted values for Co-operative/Co-operative/Teamwork is 2 + 1 + 1 = 4.

As per the above table, the final ranking of the values at all the levels put together is as on next page.

Table 14.4 Valuewise Ranking: A summary

Values	Weighted Values (Points)	Ranks
Respect/Human beings	6	I
Co-operative/Teamwork/Co-operation	4	II
Conviction	2	III
Self-Restraint/Self-Control	2	III
Creativity/Detachment/Happiness/ Fairness/Positive Attitude/Service Oriented/ Industriousness/Excellence/Results	One (each)	V

14.3 '*Quo Vadis*'?

The preceding two chapters and this chapter have given us insights about important values relevant to transforming Managers at individual and professional levels and Management at organisational level, respectively. The issue is whether these values when adhered to at different levels by management are good enough? Good enough, in terms of enabling them to transform the organisation through human values. Can transformation at individual, professional and organisational levels be considered synonymous with the transformation of the organisation as a whole?

Note: This issue will be taken up in the next chapter.

Endnotes

Saint Speak

Mother Teresa addresses Calcutta Management Association (1979)

"Management is a great work because it involves dealing with people and people need love and compassion. It is not enough just to pay them, it is not enough just to give them a job. It is something more than that. You would need to have love and respect for the person working with you and for you – for that person is your brother and your sister…..

Please love the people who are working for you for they are great people and they will love you in return. In your love that you gave them, they will give you their understanding. My prayer for you is: Love your people and that you love them until it hurts you. You cannot love unless you know them, unless they are somebody to you – they are an individual, a man, a woman created for greater thing, a child of god – my brother, my sister, and if you could realize that then your management and your firm, whatever and wherever you are will grow and bring much fruit".

Source: Calcutta management Association (CMA), Newsletter, 1979.

❑❑❑

15

Transformation of Organisation through *Spandan* 3-D Process

In the difficult times and challenging environment sometimes one feels like giving up and mind and heart shrink. With positive minds and persistent effort, one can always find life at the end of the tunnel. If your effort is more than the other people and your mind and heart is bigger, you can always overcome difficult times. It is extremely important to explore the alternatives and with purity of mind and not looking too much on some factors, one can always find truth and find a way. With innovative thinking and expanding one own mind and heart, one can conquer the world.

— **S.H. Konosuke, Matsushita**

15.1 *Spandan* Spectrum of Human Values in Work Situations

The focus of this chapter is on transformation of the organisation through human values, with the objective of having a balance between Results and Relations as a means of developing a functionally humane organisation.

Below is a table containing the salient features and findings of a survey of 396 academicians and professionals in management from India and abroad on developing and applying a spectrum of values relevant to an organisation (G.P. Rao 1996). The table contains a spectrum of 44 values, which was developed by the author through a six Phase research work: Review of Literature; Pilot study; Preliminary finalization (value dyads); field work; expert opinion; and finalization.

This study is used as reference point and the table contains relevant particulars.

Table 15.1 Human values in organisation (work situations): A spectrum

Sr. No.	Human Values	1	2	3	4	5	Total
1.	Acquiring Resources				✓		1
2.	Sharing resources				✓		1
3.	Assertiveness				✓		1
4.	Support			✓	✓		2
5.	Community Interest				✓		1
6.	Customer Demand/Orientation		✓		✓		2
7.	Controlling others				✓		1
8.	Self-control	✓			✓		2
9.	Conviction			✓	✓	✓	3
10.	Compassion			✓	✓		2
11.	Conformity				✓		1
12.	Creativity		✓	✓	✓		3
13.	Co-operation	✓	✓	✓	✓		4
14.	Competition				✓		1
15.	Democracy	✓			✓		2
16.	Discipline	✓	✓		✓		3
17.	Devotion to duty		✓		✓		2
18.	One's own needs				✓		1
19.	Emotional detachment towards benefits		✓	✓	✓		3
20.	Professional attachment towards work				✓		1
21.	Employee Performance (present)				✓		1
22.	Employee development (future)	✓			✓		2
23.	Fairness	✓			✓		2
24.	Firmness			✓	✓		2
25.	Freedom	✓			✓		2
26.	Self-Restraint		✓	✓	✓		3
27.	Happiness	✓		✓	✓		3

Sr. No.	Human Values	1	2	3	4	5	Total
28.	Prosperity				✓		1
29.	Human Beings	✓	✓	✓	✓	✓	5
30.	Rules and regulations				✓		1
31.	Material benefits			✓	✓		2
32.	Spiritual pursuits			✓	✓		2
33.	Profits				✓		1
34.	Service				✓	✓	2
35.	Relation				✓		1
36.	Results	✓	✓	✓	✓		4
37.	Shareholder's claims				✓		1
38.	Employee needs				✓		1
39.	Trusting others		✓	✓	✓		3
40.	Verifying before trusting others				✓		1
41.	Living for work				✓		1
42.	Work for living				✓	✓	2
43.	*'Quid pro quo'*				✓		1
44.	Commitment				✓		1

Table 15.2 Valuewise Ranking in Organisation (Work Situation)

Human Values	Total	Ranks
Human Beings	5	I
Co-operation	4	II
Results	4	II
Conviction	3	IV
Creativity	3	IV
Discipline	3	IV
Emotional detachment	3	IV
Self-Restraint	3	IV
Happiness	3	IV
Service	3	IV
Trusting Others	3	IV

15.2 Transformation of Management and Organisation

To answer the question, whether the transformation of manager and management can be considered as the same as that of transformation of organisation, we will compare the relevant data.

The summary table of values at Individual, Professional and Organisational levels reproduced (Chapter 14).

Table 14.4

Values	Weighted Values (Points)	Ranks
Respect/Human beings	6	I
Co-operative/Teamwork/Co-operation	4	II
Conviction	2	III
Self-Restraint/Self Control	2	III
Creativity/Detachment/Happiness/ Fairness/Positive Attitude/Service Oriented/ Industriousness/Excellence/Results	One (each)	V

When juxtaposed, the ranked statuses of the values emanating from these two tables are shown below:

Table 15.3

Rank	Managerial Transformation (Table 14.4)	Organisational Transformation (Table 15.2)
I	Respect/Human beings	Human beings
II	Co-operation	Co-operation, Results
III	Conviction, Self-Restraint/Self-control	–
IV	–	Conviction, Creativity, Discipline, Emotional detachment towards benefits, Self-restraint, Happiness, Service, Trusting Others

Three observations can be offered:

1. The number of values is not the same
2. The number of values is larger (12), in the case of Organsiational Transformation as compared to the transformation of managers at individual, Professional and Collective Level and

3. All the values are found common in both the context with, however varying ranks. Results, however, is one value which is figuring at II rank in the case of. Transformation of Organisation. This single value makes the entire difference.

This is an invaluable insight from this analysis.

To have further insights on this issue, we may bring in the value wise analysis at Individual, Professional and Management levels and compare with the corresponding ranking of organisation based values:

Table 15.4 Top Human Values at Individual, Professional and Organisational Levels and Organisational Values

Values	Individual (Table 12.2)	Professional (Table 13.2)	Organisational (Table 14.2)	Organisation (Work Situation Table 15.2)
	Co-operation	Co-operation (team work)	Co-operation	Co-operation
	Human Beings	Human Beings (Respect)	Human Beings	Human Beings
	Conviction	Conviction	–	Conviction
	Creativity	–	–	Creativity
	Self-Restraint/ Control	–	Self-Restraint/ Control	Self-Restraint/ Control
	Emotional Detachment	–	–	Emotional Detachment
	Happiness	–	–	Happiness
	–	Fairness	–	–
	–	Service Oriented	–	Service Oriented
	–	–	Industriousness, Excellence (Nearer to results), Effectiveness	Result
	–	–	–	Discipline
	–	–	–	Trusting others
No. of Top Values	6	5	4	11
No. of Ranked Values	6	6	4	11
No. of Select Values	50	14	13	44
Top Values as % of select values	12%	36%	31%	25%

The given table offers comparative analysis about the nature and scope of managerial values at Individual Professional and Organisational Levels on the one hand and of the organisation as representing work situation on the other. The table indicates that;

1. All the top ranked values at Individual and Organisational Levels were also among the top ranked values at the Organisation Level (Work Situation). Still the Organisation (Work Situation) three top values, namely Service, Discipline and Trusting Others, remain outside of the purview.

2. In the case of Professional Level values however, of the six ranked values five are among the Top values, the exception being Positive Attitude. This implies that , identifying the value of Positive Attitude as one among the select values and incorporating it in the spectrum of Work situation would strengthen the value base of the organisation.

The next table presents the ranked values at Individual Professional and Organisational Levels as integrated to the Human Values at Work Situation (Organisation).

No*	Values	Individual	Professional	Organisational	Organisation	
4	Support	✓		✓	✓	I
8	Self-control	✓		✓	✓	I, O
9	Conviction	✓		✓	✓	I, O
10	Compassion	✓		✓		I
12	Creativity	✓		✓		I
13	Co-operation	✓	✓	✓	✓	I, P, O
15	Democracy			✓		
16	Discipline	✓			✓	I
19	Emotional Detachment	✓			✓	I
22	Employee Development			✓	✓	O
23	Fairness		✓		✓	P
24	Firmness	✓			✓	I
25	Freedom	✓			✓	I
26	Self-restraint	✓			✓	I

No*	Values	Individual	Professional	Organisational	Organisation	
27	Happiness	✓			✓	I
29	Human Beings	✓	✓	✓	✓	I, P, O
31	Material Benefits		✓			✓ I
32	Spiritual Pursuits	✓			✓	I
34	Service		✓		✓	P
36	Results				✓	O
39	Trusting Others				✓	O

Endnotes

Stalwarts: ***Speak***

I. Tatas Speak

1. J.N. Tata, the founder of TISCO, Jamshedpur through a letter appeals to Swami Vivekananda that managers should spend a life of abstinence and renunciation periodically in a system like *Gurukul* for gaining composure and self-control.
2. **J.R.D. Tata**, in the public mind, business ethics is mainly connected with financial integrity. Important as that is, the real meaning of the word – 'ethics' goes far beyond. It is the "science of morals in human conduct, a moral principle or code".
3. **J.R.D. Tata:** There is a belief in our country that our culture and our character cannot allow our people to attain consistently high standards; that shoddiness and carelessness are our God-given ways of life. But if faith in them, you ask our men for their best, they rise to a belief in their work and create a momentum towards improvement. Often I have seen men who were considered ordinary, rise to extraordinary heights.
4. **J.R.D. Tata** had the guiding principle that "no success or achievement in material terms is worthwhile unless it … is achieved by fair and honest means."
5. **Ratan Tata** speaking on TATA Group's acquisition of CORUS, the anglo-dutch steel maker, in 2006, stated that TATA's first evaluate a company's value system before acquiring or merging with it "as values and human chemistry are very important to us".
6. The JRD QV (Quality Value) Award started in 1995 as a means of measurement of corporate leadership.
7. Tata Unified HR Approach since 2004 – replacing uniform approach.

II. N.R. Narayana Moorthy, Chairman and Chief Mentor, Infosys, talks to Indian School of Business (ISB) *Insight*, September 2008 – excerpts:

ISB: makes you different as a leader, on how you incorporate values and personify values ?

NM: The primary of a leader is to be a transformational agent because transformation is a big-ticket progress. And progress is positive change. Progress is what is needed to make life better for any community, any institution. So the role of the leader is to martial the resources required to achieve that transformation. A leader's main responsibility is to raise the aspirations needed, to make them more confident, to make them more enthusiastic, more energetic, to go after what appears to be plausibly impossible.....so the responsibility of the leader is to convert plausibly impossible targets into convincingly possible one.

ISB: How do you bring in emphasis on values in whatever you do?

NM: Value-Systems I would define, are the protocol for behaviour in a community where the action of every member of the community raises the confidence, the enthusiasm and the hope of every other member in the community, working towards the future of the community.

ISB: The leadership traits you have imbibed – inspired by Lee Kuan Yew, former Singapore Prime Minister – for yourself ?

NM: Courage, firmness, trust and "the walking the talk"

ISB: How a firm can contribute to society and why?

NM: It is the society that contributes customers to a firm. It is the society that contributes employees to the firm. It is the society investors; people buy your shares. It is the society that contributes bureaucracy and political leadership who influence your policy. So if you don't create goodwill with the society and you don't leave in harmony with the society then it will be difficult for you to attract good customers, good employees and good investors..... No corporation can exist in the luxury of isolation.

ISB: How to incorporate social values in a company? Can we measure it?

NM: For Infosys, motto was to be the most respected company in India, now changed to become a globally respected corporation that delivers best – in – class, end to end business solutions, leveraging technology and employing best of breed professionals. Measurement, Feeling belonged and proud to be part of the given organisation.

ISB: Starting as an entrepreneur to a company that you are today – how did you handle this transformation?

NM: The key issue is, conduct yourself well, lead by example in the group that you are interacting closely with and then make sure that they set those examples and practice those values.

❑❑❑

16

Community Service as a Human Value and Institution Building: A Study of Jaipur Rugs Company, Jaipur

Servanthood is the chief modifier of the power implicit in all leadership. – a quality of innerness, an attribute of soul that checks the corruptibility of power .... Real power is always an exchange of leadership to use power to call out the God-given power of others.

— **Bennett J. Sims**

The title, or at least a part of it, of this chapter could as well have been 'Power of ONE'. It is about a person without any affluence, high education or political or social connections. What distinguishes him from others is unflinching faith in the basic goodness of others; and an obsession to help the weaving community come up in their lives. Nand Kishore Chaudhary, the Founder Director of Jaipur Rugs Co. Pvt. Ltd., Jaipur had in fact to pay a price. This was in terms of severe upheavals in the growth of the company.

Instead of losing faith in others, he became selective in trusting others. Families of weaving community spread over the country are closely involved with his company. Since they belong to the lowest strata of society, Chaudhary thought, it is his responsibility to help them come up in their lives as a token to his appreciation to their contribution. As a result, the company has become a world class leader and Chaudhary has become a legion in terms of receiving accolades from his fellow industry men and academicians from different parts of the world.

Before we hear the institution builder, we may have an idea on what the institution building is.

16.1 Institution Building: A Perspective

The quality of institutions and its leaders in the given country is considered as a measure of the potential and actual level of its growth. M.J. Robinson, for instance, states that "Everyday society must teach itself and its young, that its basic values are good, and its institutions are appropriate for achieving those values. In other words, each society, pluralistic, or monolithic, must peddle legitimacy, it is this belief in and commitment to the values and institutions – it is legitimacy – that allows a nation to transcend brief crises or endure long periods of deprivation." The number, emergence, range, and functioning are some of the issues which are involved in the process of institution building. As can be noted, such institution building is closely related to concepts like management like planning, organizing, directing and controlling, as also functional aspects of management like production, finance, marketing and personnel, it has a close bearing with management. To the extent, institution building involves creation of an institution with the required vision, commitment, conviction, and risk taking attitude, institution building has a built in component of Entrepreneurship.

Finally, to the extent it is the quality of leadership particularly at the apex level – which becomes instrumental in the creation, functioning, and growth of the given institution; institution building is equally organically related to leadership. It may perhaps be appropriate to quote, in this context, R. Baum Hart, S.J. who stated that usually a company is the lengthened shadow of one man- the chief executive. One can thus note that the concept of institution building is almost co extensive with the concepts of management, entrepreneurship and leadership. I however, do feel that institution building is something different and broader phenomenon. Based on whatever little experience I have in being associated with the building of a department of an institution of higher learning, I believe that institution building involves an eternal struggle between balancing contradictory objectives.'

- Vision vs. Pragmatism;
- Conviction vs. Adaptivness;
- Commitment vs. Self-sacrifice;
- Idealism vs. Flexibility;
- Perfectionism vs. One man show; and
- Institution vs. Individual.

We will find several of the above issues and dilemmas faced by Chaudhary and his organisation Jaipur Rugs in the pages to follow.

16.2 The Institution Builder: An Autobiographical Retrospective

Meet Nanda Kishore Chaudhary, the proponent of this chapter. Let us have him in his own words."I will start this note with an important event in my life that I still remember. I was studying B. Com. in Lohia College, Churu (Rajasthan). One day one of our professors while reading the role numbers in class asked me to stand up as he read my role number. This professor was known to be a hard taskmaster and strict disciplinarian. I was not sure why I was asked to stand up and got bit scared. The professor said that this boy will become a big business man one day. He opened my examination answer sheet and read out aloud the definition of the 'business' that I had written in that answer sheet. I had written, "Business is next to love. It is creator and preserver of civilizations." This was my first thought and understanding about business world. I accepted this definition as it is till date. I was just 20 years old then.

I remember one more event that occurred even before this. I was 18 years old then and was studying in college. My father was cloth merchant. I was used to sit at times with him in his shop. One day my college librarian visited the shop and bought some cloths on credit from me. After few days he again came back and bough some more cloths on credit with the promise that he would make full payment when he receives his next salary. But he did not make the due payment even after passing of many days. This made me really sad and I was bit depressed. My father was not at all happy with me. I was a very simple person who was used to trust every person.

I made a similar mistake in 2006 also. I was suffering from Urine Infection. One person whom I was used to trust very much asked for Rs. 2 lacs from me assuring that he would get me the right treatment for this infection. But he cheated with me and ran away with the money.

■ Diagnosis

As I went along I came across many good and bad incidents. These incidents helped me to deepen understanding of life. With every failure I made a promise to myself to try to understand the human nature. I attended many HR seminars, interacted with professional experts, read autobiographies, many other books and magazines. This helped me understand me how to manage my relation with others. I distanced myself from people who were not trustworthy. I shared my experiences with my children and tried to educate them about different aspects of a business. Along with my children, I tried to involve many honest and dedicated people with me in my business.

■ Discovery

The one understanding that I have reached to is that there is no better decision than 'team-decision'. Team brings Collective Wisdom in any decision.

I have also improved on my capability of selecting right people for my business. Few days back I along with a team was interviewing a candidate for the position of accountant. I felt that he is trying to hide something. When we did a background check of that candidate we came to know his record was very negative in the last company.

■ Development

When I was 5 years old, I was used to trust every human being. I still trust every human but with some constructive thought and analysis. In my younger days I was not good in analysis. By analysis I mean an ability to identify the right individual. This was my weakness. I was not good in selecting right individual with whom I should work. But on the other side my trust on every human being helped me to reach where I have reached today. I loved and trusted my weavers, customers and employees. This love and trust has brought me and my company where we are today. The decisions that I was used to take myself are now being arrived at through a capable team.

From my childhood only, I never liked the ostentatious and deceptive nature of People. I never liked people of such nature and they also did not like me When I was just 14 years old that time I was used to talk of value in business rather than profit. Many people that time said about me that I will never be able to make any money. They were used to preach me about concentrating on profit not value. When I was getting married around the age of 25, I refused to ask for Dowry. This made my parents very angry. Similar incidents distanced me from my family members. Finally I became indifferent to them.

My father was into business and mother was home maker. I have one brother and four sisters.

Today one of the biggest challenge in front of me is to incorporate social values and ideals in my business that I have learnt and follow myself. I want to establish these values as a work culture in my company so that every individual in my company could become a decision maker."

16.3 His Basic Beliefs

1. Love is ultimate value in our society but without market label, price and tagging system. It has been a part of Values. On the other hand, commitment comes from love and affection, always.
2. In the present market scenario, love seems a secondary part of life.
3. We have to start the work with ourselves – that means self analysis; and then acceptance comes automatically. By analyzing ourselves, we can see the world as it is. This is the only thing that makes the difference.
4. HR does the work like a mother, who knows everything about her child without asking anymore.
5. Finally, values are the roots of every business.

16.4 The Growth of the Company

The company has gone through two phases since its inception in 1978 and is currently going through the third phase.

- The First Phase (1978–1986) when the company was engaged in job work.
- The Second Phase (1986–1999), when the focus was on exports done through previous company Exports.
- The Third Phase (1999–till date), when the organisation assumed the role of 'Intrapreneurship. Through Jaipur Rugs Foundation, the company offers training to the needy young ambitious and talented youngsters and encourages and supports them to stand on their own feet.

The tables (on page 146) provide phase wise data on sales, production, no. of branches, employees and artisan's. The tables reveal that the growth has been phenomenal – an increase between 7 to 8 folds in terms of sales revenue and production area. More important however, is the sense of pride in ones own worth instilled in the artisans and trainers in carpet weaving.

16.5 Service to the Weaving Community

In a document entitled 'Case Studies', the company recounts success stories of four individuals and their families belonging to the weaving community. These case studies reinforce what has been stated above regarding instilling self pride in the ambitious but struggling youth in search of their real worth to themselves and to others.

Particulars	Job Work	Phase 1 Previous Company Export	Jaipur Rugs	Job Work	Phase 2 Previous Company Export	Jaipur Rugs	Job work	Phase 3 Previous Company Export	Jaipur Rugs
Avg. Sales (Rs. in Lacs)	2.89	376.22	855.37	20.48	1167.78	1813.12	109.73	2539.03	3798.05
Avg. No. of Branches	1	7	1	3	9	6	5	10	13
Avg. Production (Sq. Ft)	962	107490	123571	5983	333650	426367	31350	741438	900150
Avg. No. of Employees	1	54	31	6	53	135	22	214	145
Avg. No. of Artisian	15	1278	6125	84	3517	11000	415	7050	19967

Phase Wise Comparison

Particulars	Job Work (1978 to 1986)			Previous Company Export (1986 to 1999)			Jaipur Rugs (1999 to till date)		
	Phase 1	Phase 2	Phase 3	Phase 1	Phase 2	Phase 3	Phase 1	Phase 2	Phase 3
Avg. Sales (Rs.in Lacs)	2.89	20.48	109.73	376.22	1167.78	2539.03	855.37	1813.12	3798.05
Avg. No. Of Branches	1	3	5	7	9	10	1	6	13
Avg. Production (Sq. Ft)	962	5983	31350	107490	333650	741438	123571	426367	900150
Avg. No. of Employees	1	6	22	54	53	214	31	135	145
Avg. No. of Artisan	15	84	415	1278	3517	7050	6125	11000	19967

Entrepreneur as a Job Work – 1978 to 1986

Entrepreneur as an Export – 1986 to 1999

Entrepreneur as an Intrapreneur – 1999 to till date

These success stories are about the youngsters with social inhibitions, economic deprivation and lack of freedom for girls. During their struggles they came to know about Jaipur Rugs Foundation and were trained and provided with looms to be economically independent and support their kith and kin.

The document is appended at the end of the book.

16.6 Nomination of the Nanda Kishore Chaudhary and his Company, Jaipur Rugs Co. Pvt. Ltd. for the Spandan IBA Award, 2007

On invitation from Spandan, Nanda Kishore Chaudhary, participated in the annual award on Human Values for Professionals, in 2007, instituted by Spandan, in collaboration with the Indian Business Academy (IBA), Greater Noida, India. The write up submitted by Chaudhary, along with the nomination for the award is reproduced below, and offers further insights into his personality and functioning.

Our Values and Humanity by Nand Kishore Chaudhary

Bill Clinton, once rightly said, "As we become ever more diverse, we must work harder to unite our common values and our common humanity". I was once a witness to the downfall of my own business that I had set up after years of struggle and sacrifices. My instant reaction was – How could it be? Life throws up challenges at times that we cannot understand. Today, if you ask me the meaning of business, I would describe it as any activity that is divine and is a source of knowing your inner self. Once we know, who we really are, we can enlighten the stakeholders of the business.

With time, I realized the points of connections in my business – the end users and the weavers. Having reached a stage today, where I easily claim that Jaipur Rugs Co. Pvt. Ltd., is a world class leader in rug category, it took me years to identify the missing the element: *the el*ement of weaver's joy and customer's satisfaction. The philosophy that crawled its way inside me was – find yourself through losing yourself!

From the very beginning, I had seen this industry fragmented. There were gaps in terms of availability of skilled labour and the middlemen never helped these weavers. These men of god went poorer day by day not even realizing their true potential of getting a sustained living. There were times when these weavers who knew the art very well were unemployed for a very long time because the middlemen did not have contracts to give them.

When I was a child, I always wanted to see a community of equal opportunities where everyone earned what they deserved and had a sustained livelihood. Today, Jaipur Rugs, follows a social entrepreneurship model, wherein , each weaver who gets in touch with us, earns considerably well in the industry; is aware of schemes or government aids and is groomed to be a future leader. I have learned from my experiences to see the world as it is, rather than applying my own set of assumptions and perceptions to survive.

Conscientiousness is the characteristic I improved upon. To understand what a customer wants and link it with a weaver's agony has a long journey. The same is imbibed within the organisational culture. From a departmental head, who takes strategic decisions to a labour that transports rugs from different centers, all of this are on the stage of learning to understand the two connections that I have stated. Once this is strived, processes automatically become efficient and by the end of the day, we keep both, weavers and customers happy.

It is more important to know what your customer thinks, where does he think, who will produce, how will he produce and how can we help them link. Through our social initiative, Jaipur Rugs Foundation, we have touched more than, 40,000 lives across 10 states in India. It is not about providing employment to the underprivileged or unemployed youths, but developing them to see their own future in the industry. Virtues of self discipline and hard work always help one to find success. However, I believe that it is the journey of success which is important and not the end result.

Now that we have a huge network of weavers and are still growing on the mission to develop a secure community, I look back and think: is it the revenues that matter or thousand smiles on these faces? The answer has been given by all these weavers who dedicatedly knot beautiful and elegant rugs. Their consistency in deliverance and their sheer determination to meet deadlines state how much they care about what they deliver. Some weavers are now entrepreneurs in their villages and this is our very next step. We are developing true leaders who will some day change the future of this industry. Thus, if we are to go forward, we must go back and rediscover those values that all reality hinges on moral foundations and that all reality has spiritual control. With this, I believe that human values are not a matter of discussion but a constant endeavour of practice.

16.7 Awards and Recognition

- In the year 1993–94 received Gold Medal from Ministry of Textiles.
- In the year 1998–99 received Gold Memento from Ministry of Textiles.
- In the year 2003–04 received Export Excellence award from Chief Minister of Rajasthan.

- In the year 2005–06 received Gold Memento from Ministry of Textiles.
- In the Year 2008–09 received Udyog Ratna Award from former Governor of Tamilnadu and Assam.

■ Invitations

Nov 15th, 2008: Lecture on Social Entrepreneurship at Wharton School, the University of Pennsylvania USA.

Nov 17th, 2008: Lecture on Social Entrepreneurship at University of Michigan USA.

March 16th, 2009: J.K. Business School, Gurgaon (Haryana)as Guest faculty.

March 25th, 2009: Amity University, Jaipur as Guest faculty.

Frequent Participation in CII & AIMA, Institutions like IILM, Jaipur , IRMA Gujarat etc.

16.8 A Personal Note

The author knows Nand Kishore Chaudhary since 2001, when Chaudhary associated himself with *Spandan* for introducing value orientation in his organisation. As an individual he is simple, unassuming and open, this gets reflected in his interactions with his family, his employees and other. What distinguishes him further is his spiritual attitude towards men and matter. He has a tendency to look beyond his family and company interests. Another important trait in him is his lack of rancor, even towards those who have harmed him in the past. This is reflected in the re-employment of a family member in a key position, who was instrumental in the downfall of his company in the past.

Finally, his vision is reflected in his current endeavors of imparting training to deserving persons in carpet weaving through Jaipur Rugs Foundation and promoting research at international level on orientation of values in the society.

Appendix: Success Stories of Weavers – appended after Epilogue.

❑❑❑

PART IV

A Viewing Point:
Beyond Management of Organisations

This part goes beyond the management of organisations. Society and World have been selected as frames of reference. **Chapter 17** examines the role of family and education in the orientation of values and their adherence in management and industry. Further, it is argued that the proper role of management in the society is to widen the role of corporate citizenship into that of an organisational citizenship. The next chapter (**Chapter 18**) focuses on the issues of the management interface with globalization and the mankind's interface with mankind. Globalisation calls for global corporate mindset with corresponding values to be integrated in work ethic and culture. Spiritual democracy recognizes the innate divinity in human beings; and thus becomes a logical corollary of our efforts at conducting ourselves befitting the spiritual dimension of human beings.

17

Management and Society:
Family, Education and Organisational Citizenship

The divine never let you down. I have an abiding faith in the Divine, which does not call for performing any rituals. See yourself as an instrument of the Divine and do everything as its instrument. Success will not then raise you to dizzying heights nor will adversity leave you in darkness. You will thereby remain God's instrument.

— **Jit Paul**

This book is on humanising at two broad levels. One is humanising management (Point of View); and, the other humanising mankind (Viewing Point). As discussed (Chap. 10), family, education and the citizen role have an important place in humanising at both the levels. We now accordingly look at these three issues.

17.1 Family and Family Values

Family is an important institution in the society. It is the institution which provides security, stability, sustenance and growth. Is it the socializing agent in terms of propagating and inculcating values, particularly during the formative years of an individual. It is the institution which provides manpower to the different segments of social, political and economic activities. Family values, particularly in the east, influence the professional and organisational values as much as individual values. The professionalism in management has to reckon with and integrate suitable family values in the culture and functioning of an organisation.

The industries in India appear to be involved in this process of integrating family values with the organisational functioning.

One method is integration of the family values with the mission statement.

Some of the leading industrial organisations in this respect are Tata group, Sahara India Parivaar, Modi Care Ltd., and Daewoo Motors India Ltd.

The role of Tata group in the integrations of family values with the mission has been covered earlier.

Sahara India Parivaar, Lucknow, indicates the importance given to the spirit of family since Parivaar means family in Hindi. The company describes itself as emotionally integrated family. All promoters, shareholders, directors and partners are from the workers rank and on oath NOT to share ever company's profits or assets. Collective materialism is another feature of the company, which is responsible for continuous collective growth for collective caring and sharing- the core of the work philosophy of the Parivaar.

Modi Care Ltd. is the first and largest direct selling brand in healthcare in India, with a motto, 'To Make a Difference'. The young President of the company, Sameer Modi, states that 'the new buzz word of corporate governance of the company is *AZADI*, (freedom, autonomy)'. It means building the company, not only financially, but also the business's main capital assets, Human Resources. The atmosphere of openness and camaraderie, characteristic of a family is used as a important tool for the purpose. He continues, "There is no discrimination of any kind in our organisation….my ultimate objective is to replace the 'I' with the 'we'……..I believe that great companies are built on the strength of the power they can harness from their human capital…….As an employer you should know what balance to strike between your brain and heart. Do not always look at how much money you can make, but how much value you can create."

Daewoo Motors India Ltd., S.G. Awasthi, Chairman states that, "*Parivartan*, or changing mindsets is the buzzword of his company; the focus is on transparency, improvement of interpersonal and interdepartmental co-ordination and creation of a family environment".

The other method being adopted is what has come to be known as internal branding. The focus is on creating and strengthening positive image of the employees of the company towards its standing and status in the society. It includes creating a relaxed, non-formal and open ambiance in the company and making the formal structure congruent to the same. Open door policy is an example of formal method. As stated however, it is the informality within the organisation that is given priority. As can be noted, unlike external branding where the attention is on consumers and the image of the company in the society in general. The realization that, external branding by itself was necessary but not sufficient till the corresponding positive perception is held within. It is said, that internal branding can be more effective than any number of advertisement put together.

Sabrina Mukund, an employee of Infosys BPO, expressed her feelings on her company's organizing fun activities which involved not only the employees but their families too. She felt, that because of these activities remembers that 'That I am an human being first and then an employee, that creates a sense of belongingness'.

Family values do influence managerial decision making at critical points of time, during crisis in particular. Jet Airways, as an example resorted to retrenchment of 1900 employees because of the economic meltdown which started at the end of 2008. Later, the decision was revoked. While announcing the decision of reinstatement of these sacked employees, Naresh Goyal, the Chairman of the company stated that he had been mentally disturbed because of the retrenchment, calling it the most emotional day of his life, he said, 'My daughter is 19 years old, they (the sacked employee) are 20 or so. I cannot see their trauma or agony'.

17.2 Education and Orientation of Values

Spandan describes itself as a Foundation for Human Values in Management and Society. Accordingly, the objective is to facilitate orientation of values in Management and Society. The implication is that an inadequate or improper balance of values in management and society will be suboptimal. The result could be inconsistency, incongruence and incompatibility leading to chaos and disorder in both. However, the role of society in balance is much higher since management is the subsystem of society. As discussed, it is the society which becomes the framework for the three vital aspects of management, namely: Management as a Resource, as a Class and as a System of Authority. The quality of education system of the given society thus becomes an important determinant of the quality of its management and organisational values.

The primary function of education is to transmit or pass on to the new generation a particular way of life (Orin Graff and Calvin M Street, 1956). The role of education can in developing a particular way of life in the society can therefore hardly be exaggerated. The National Committee of Enquiry into Higher Education, 1997, UK, stated that 'in the next century, the economically successful nations will be those which become learning societies, where all are committed effective education and training to lifelong learning.

Relevant to the frame of reference of humanising people, a particular way of life which education can seek is how to humanise people. Value based education has had been developed and developing as a response. All societies have evolved schemes of imparting education especially for the young, keeping ideals and utility as the ingredients of learning programme. Jesuits are the pioneers in this respect and have had the conscious to look deeper into the man's unique activity called learning which is the process of development of his life through knowledge.

The education – formal in particular does not appear to have served its purpose.

Education however, does not stop at producing literate persons with mere knowledge, but to develop lettered individuals with wisdom as value addition. The issue however does not stop here, existence of sound education does not necessarily mean that the young one's are being oriented properly. We need individuals with strong convictions and deep knowledge as mentors and role models. Teachers must therefore acquire proper mindsets through suitable training and individual development programmes.

The youth, it is felt, is resistant to values based education. The experience of the author as a teacher through out his life however indicates that one has at least to reexamine this issue. Generally the students, particular at the tender age of primary education, when they start formal education , which is our focus here are highly sensitive and inquisitive. They are intellectually curious and emotionally open enough to understand, appreciate and adopt thing which they consider desirable.

This facet of younger generation had come out in groups of school children who participated in contests held by two prestigious new papers in the country.

The Hindu carried a lead article on April 2, 1994 entitled: "The India I would like to live in" The write up contained excerpts from select letters received from school going children on the topic. Twenty six such excerpts were published. A few of them were much mundane and down to earth. One such letter, 'Life a bore', is a good example of a typical child's dread about school and school teachers. As I enter the school gate, I feel I am entering a prison. No liberty to talk or play as I like. No time to stand and stare at any thing." One is almost reminded of scenes from a novel of Charles Dickens!

Most of the letters were highly idealistic, emotional, patriotic and universe-oriented, if one may say so Some typical captions were: No barbed wire fence; No backward classes; No fear or furore; and No discrimination. 'Men of substance' and 'Lion-hearted men' were some expressions used to describe perhaps their role models. One letter however merits special mention. Entitled, 'India of yore', the letter opens with "Given a choice, I would like to live in a value based society. The modern India has disappointed the youth."

After nearly fifteen years, Times of India asked kids on the eve of Children's Day on November 14, 2008 to tell the one thing they would like to change in the world today. The Lead titled, What children want, carried nine statements.

Here also, at least one child was very clear and down to earth in what he wants. He declares, "I would like to change the timings of my school. It's difficult to wake up early in the morning"!

The other eight children whose views were published were however no less idealistic and noble than their predecessors of down south who voiced their dreams around fifteen years ago at which time most of these eight children from this part of the country would not have born. Region being different, time being different, social and economic settings perhaps being different, the children's voice, longing and dream remains the same and one and the same. As C. Langar says, "Make the world more sensitive towards human values".

The Search Institute, a Minneapolis, USA based independent research group undertook a project for two years involving around 7000 youths, ages 12-25, in 17 countries has explored Spiritual Beliefs and Experiences. The institute released the initial findings of the survey in November, 2008. The vast majority of respondents shared a conviction that life has a spiritual dimension. 75% believed in God or a higher power. While some could not easily define spirituality, the majority said that they had a transcendent experience, believed in life after death and thought it was probably true that all living things were connected. The above empirical data indicates the innate interest of the present youth in spirituality and an inclination towards a spiritual life. The issue therefore is to, how best to translate their inclination to action. The responsibility primarily lies with the others – educators, particularly in the present context.

17.3 Education as Change Agent

Let us assume, that the young generation has an open mind and inclination to adopt and adapt values which they consider desirable. Hence, it should be easier for the education institutions to facilitate them to become better human beings. Albert Einstein quotes,

> "Try not to become a man of success but rather to become a man of values".

Enabling the students become value oriented individuals involves two basic tasks from the educational institutions. The first is with reference to the educators and the second is relating to the education institutions.

How to 'Teach' values is the issue to be grappled with by educators. The values, it may be reiterated, cannot be 'taught', in the sense that, 'Knowledge is transmitted and skills are imparted'. The only way to teach values is through the behaviour of the teacher. The behaviour should be perceived by the students as one of genuine and authentic of the teacher as a person. This perception of authenticity is a function of the consistency over a period of time in the communication and the conduct of the teacher. This consistency in turn is a function of the conviction with which the teacher upholds and adheres to the values, which he considers to be taught to the students. The interconnectedness and congruence needed between and among Possession, Projection and Perception thus comes to the fore.

The 'teaching' of values is therefore to be leading and example and by being a role model by the teacher. Such teaching therefore is to be perceived as a natural self of the teacher and should be as inconspicuous as possible. In that sense, teaching values resembles to the mythical invisible river 'Saraswati', as compared to Knowledge and Skills being the rivers Ganga and Yamuna.

Educator being or becoming an effective role model to impart values is necessary but not sufficient. The educational institution of which he is a part and through, he/she acts as a catalyst for change should equally be perceived as an values oriented institution. In the present context of 'Corporatisation' of education, it may rather be difficult to become congruent with the traditional image of school being a 'temple'. There are however institutions which really aim at to become 'model organisations', as part of their institution building.

When these two conditions are fulfilled, then, suitable curriculum and learning process is to be evolved and implemented. Further, as mentioned, the teachers should be trained to acquire the required mindset to become the role models. *Spandan*, as an example, is attempting such training and development activities for teachers and other constituents like management and students.

17.4 The Role of the Organisation as an Organisation Citizen

The management and organisation are part of the society. They have accordingly certain rights flowing from their being a part of the society and responsibilities towards the society for the same reason.

Earliest approach was that business of business is business, implying that so long the organisation, abided by the rules of the land, their job is over. Philanthropic organisations, however looked into the needs of their employees only on humanitarian grounds.

The second phase occurred after the World War I and II and their consequent upheavals on the world, politically, economically, educationally and culturally. As a result, assuming social responsibility was considered necessary. This included doing good for the community in which the organisations were located.

The third phase happened, when most of the countries, particularly in the developing world, attained freedom. Being independent and developing, the challenges facing these countries were two fold: 1. Economic Development and 2. Social Justice. Production of wealth and distribution of wealth were to be balanced. The responsibilities of the industries towards their country and economy have gone through radical changes. The trade unions, government and public opinion formed powerful centers of regulations and influence on modifying the roles of industry in a developing country. As a result, several efforts at the levels of management and organisations, government, world agencies and NGO's evolved several modes of course of conduct, informal and otherwise.

The fourth and current phase, relates to the changed role of management in the context of globalization and its impact on the world. The problems of unequal distribution of wealth within the countries and across the countries got accentuated. Consequently, conducts of ethics and values at global level are assuming greater and greater importance.

As on date, a quick perusal of current scenario indicates the following codes and other methods of ethical and value oriented behaviour:

- Business Ethics
- Corporate Social Responsibility
- Corporate Governance
- Corporate Philanthropy
- Corporate Citizenship
- Integrity packed (of Transparency International Global Corruption Watchdog)
- Social Accountability 8000 (SA 8000) – launched by Council of Economic Priorities Accreditation Agency (CEPAA)
- Corporate's Conscience
- Inclusive Growth

Keeping the framework of human values of the book and India being a developing country where rural India (also called as Bharat) needs special attention, two suggestions are offered.

The first suggestion relates to the values dimension of the concept of corporate citizenship. Corporate Citizenship is an idea and a philosophy which has both ethical and economic dimensions. It advocates doing right things. It gives more importance to means then to end. Companies have rights and responsibilities *vis a vis* the commitment which the corporate's seek to serve.

It has been observed that in practice, the implementation of Corporate Citizenship was assuming greater and greater legal outlook and formalism. The spirit of being voluntary had thus been eroded. Observers like Arun Mehra feel that the organisations should have greater look within themselves as part of compliance with the concept. Therefore, the managers and management as the catalyst of change in their own organisations are expected to change their mindset and that of others accordingly.

The second suggestion relates to the change in the name of the concept and widening accordingly the scope of its operations. The first part of the concept in corporate citizenship – intentionally or otherwise excludes the non-corporate organized sector, unorganized sector and activities outside of industrial sphere. The relevance and importance of such a code is if anything, is higher. Accordingly, it should be called as Organisational Citizenship, thereby implying that all the organisation in the country, have in principle same set of responsibilities towards the society and the country. The other aspect is about the widening of the application. Rural sector, being predominant, the organisations need to look into the development of villages. APJ Abdul Kalam, the former President of India, had been advocating Integrated Partnership for Development with a critical role to the corporate sector. He states that, 'the corporate sector should go beyond its responsibilities to employees and customers and undertake activities of social responsibilities like establishing Providing Urban Amenities in Rural Areas (PURA), in its neighbourhood.

Endnotes

1. Corporate Executive in India – Certain Facets
   (*a*) An average corporate executive is teetotaler, traditional, god fearing and family oriented who prefers a lesser hectic social life: Results of survey conducted by NFOMBL India Ltd. among people belonging to the age group of 24–50 years in 2002
   (*b*) Indian business leaders are among the world's most stressed employees as they put in more working hours (57 hrs/week), in a bid to remain competitive in a globalised and technologically advance world: Grand Thornton International Business Report (IBR), 2007. The survey tracks the attitudes and expectations of small and medium size businesses, consisting of the opinions of 7200 privately owned businesses in 32 countries.
   (*c*) Professionals in India excel when it comes to activities and profession that involve logical and analytical thinking. These left brain professionals are known to develop the depth of thinking. But when it comes to right brain profession like art, sports and philosophy which develop our breadth of thinking they struggle.
2. The Lok Sabha resolution adopted in 1997 on the occasion of the Golden Jubilee of Independence. The resolution develops agenda for India and refers to minimum task for the purpose; 'that the national economy be prudently managed with emphasis on efficient use of generation of wealth and balanced regional development.
3. Guide Posts for the future of India: R.A. Mashelkar, the then Director General CSIR, New Delhi, proposed guide posts for the future of India at the convocation address of IIT New Delhi in 1999. He states that a 5 point millennium agenda linking child, women, the human, the society and the nation, to put them on fast track development in the next century. These are child-centered education; women centered family; human-centered development; knowledge-entered societies and innovation-centered India.

4. Jawaharlal Nehru, on progress: Progress does not ultimately consist of merely industrial enterprises. That is only a symbol it. Progress ultimately has to be measured by the quality of human beings, how they are improving, how their lot is improving and how they are adopting themselves to modern ways and yet keep their feet firmly planted on their soil.
5. Integrated Partnership for Development: APJ Abdul Kalam, the former President of India, proposes integrated partnership for development on the occasion of Republic Day in 2007. The constituents are political leaders; law makers – MP's and MLA's; administrators; police, lawyers; judges; corporate sector; religious/spiritual leaders, citizens. Abdul Kalam declares that all the constituents and the personalities involved have to be transparent and pure, then only an integrated partnership for development can emerge.
6. Baha'i Principles of Development: Baha'i International Community has annunciated in 1998 spirituality based indicators for the development of India along with corresponding priority policy areas in which these can be applied;

Spirituality Based Indicator	**Priority Policy Area**
Unity in Diversity	Economic Development
Equity and Justice	Education
Equality of the sexes	Environmental Stewardship
Trustworthiness and Moral Leadership	Meeting basic needs in Food, Nutrition, Health and Shelter
Independent Investigation of Truth	Governance and Participation

❑❑❑

18

Management and the World

> *Indians have a special, and perhaps unique, faculty for adjusting themselves to foreign ways without themselves ceasing to be characteristically Indian.*
>
> — J. Duncan M. Derrell

Beyond management of organsiations, three supra systems exist: Society; World; and the Universe. The preceding chapter dealt with society. In this chapter, we look at two select aspects of human functioning at global level. One, management interface with globalisation; and, the other mankind interface with mankind.

18.1 Management and Globalisation

Nirmalya Kumar, London Business School, London comes out with certain insights on the process of globalization in India and its impact on management (2009). Acording to Nirmalya Kumar, the transformation of Indian companies from domestic to global players occurred in three phases. Pre reforms, prior 1991, Indian business was in shackles. The institutionalized environment of licensing and limited competition led to domestic success without developing the unique competencies, the resources, or the viable scale necessary for competitive advantage to the international markets.

The second phase, post-1991, economic reform necessitated decade – long corporated restructuring to make companies globally competitive. This phase has four essential elements: cleaning the balance sheet, improving competitiveness, focusing on core businesses, and strengthening management. In that decade, Indian companies having quest to go global, had to grapple with three issues about overcoming the mindset barrier: making a leap of faith, persistence in the face of initial setbacks and overcoming the liabilities of 'Made in India' origin.

During the current, third phase, Indian companies are increasingly going global. These companies have learnt that to obtain orders at global level, having low prices was not sufficient. In addition, four other methods were found necessary and useful: having world-class capabilities (assets, processes and knowledge); acquiring a dominant lever; transformational merger; and, utilization of India-specific product competencies to enter other emerging markets.

That globalization has not been an flawless process has been recognized even by its proponents and staunch supporters. Corrective measures are being undertaken at the levels of government and international agencies with the motto of globality, *i.e.*, managing the undesirable consequences of globalisation. Their efforts are complimented by Global Civil Society Organisations (GCSOs), by instituting normative discourses in international forums. The efforts of these societies have however by and large globalised political and civil rights but not social and economic rights. Their vision has not transcended the norms of powerful western states. As a result, the developing countries remained poorer in all respects. Over a period of time, the benefits of globalization got distributed skewed in the favor the developed countries. Consequently, the developing countries became poorer and poorer.

From the perspective of human values as means for facilitating management meet the challenges of globalization, as indicated by Nirmalya Kumar, certain requisites appear to be important. Speaking about the experience of Birla Group of Industries going global, its Chairman, Kumarmangalam Birla, stated that there are five determinants for a company to acquire the characteristics of a global organisation. The first is 'developing corporate mindset means the willingness to integrate which involves a great tussle between the intellectual conviction that they have to act local, and the ingrain comfort of doing it the way thy have always done it'. (2) "To make your people understand and respect local habits, cultures etc."; (3) " Establish brand equity overseas" ; (4) " To develop a global pool of management talent" and (5)" To makes one's globalised character successful and sustainable". Applying this statement to Birla Group, he states that, "what bonds us, are our values – integrity, speed, seamlessness, commitment and passion. We expect these values to define the character of our corporation and serve as a guiding principle for employees. Our values are a moral contract between he employees and the organisation. A contract that goes beyond business and economic transactions".

Taking the above five requisites as representative of a typical Indian orgnaisation assume the role of an Indian Multi national Corporation, we may try to have a quick look at the situation obtainable in our country at present.

- Global Corporate Mindset: The managers are required to assume knew knowledge skills and attitudes for the purpose. Indian managers are known for their intellect, hard work, and sincerity of purpose. If anything, Indian managers need to develop their social skills. Generally they are strong in analytical abilities and decision making skills, it is the soft skills that they need to work up on.

- At the work group level, managers in India need to develop their ability to work in teams. As has been found by S.K. Chakraborty, team spirit is an important value in Indian cultural milieu, but which happens to be the weakest in management.

  "The organisationl value most cherished, yet wanting in India today is teamwork. The real answer to this gap to develop the inner conviction and feel about one's true identity to be the Self and self. Work from the plane of Self perception shall lead us to see unity in diversity". (For an excellent discussion on the role of cross border business teams, reference may be made to Anil K. Gupta *et al.*, "The quest for Global Dominance", 2008)

- With reference to understanding and respecting local habits and cultures, a different set of values become relevant. These are openness and flexibility. It may be noted that the list of 13 values of Global leaders developed by Ed. Cohen gives due importance to these values.

- The organisational responsibilities of building brand equity, pool of management talent and its globalised character are the responsibility of the management as a team. What is however relevant here is *Spandan* approach of emphasizing basic goodness in human beings and its 3-D process aiming at developing a Functionally Humane Organisation, is an effort is this direction. It may offer suitable leads for a corporate to create an organisation with an optimal balance between Results and Relations.

It may however be significant to note that developing a value oriented organisation is not anything great or something new or the management to be crow about. The reason is any orgnaisation has to be value oriented. As stated by JRD Tata, "In the public mind, business ethics is mainly connected with financial integrity. Important as that is, the real meaning of the word 'ethics' goes far beyond that. It is the science of morals in human conduct, a moral principle or code".

S.K. Chakraborty observes that "values do not enter into management as something foreign to its nature, something that may give it, at best, a moral polish. Values inhere in true management and work as the spring of all energy behind the operations of the organisation. They give dignity to the individual and personality to the corporate body."

Further reflection would reveal that the need to be value oriented, is not specific to a particular category of people like management, but applies to other profession, spheres of activity and humanity as a whole.

In the context of the ideological upheavals and turmoils which the world is witnessing and experiencing over a period of time, the only and perhaps the real answer is to elevate ourselves from the lower sense of pettiness to higher sense of dignity and divinity. We may recall, the words of Jacquelyn Small, American spiritual psychologist, "We are not small human beings trying to be spiritual; we are spiritual beings practicing to be human". Spiritual democracy then, is a logical corollary of our efforts at conducting ourselves befitting the spiritual dimension of human being.

18.2 Spiritual Democracy

Based on *Vedantic* philosophy, Spiritual Democracy entails "the recognition of divinity in every man and woman" as well as "everybody's inherent right to liberation or *moksha*". Such spiritual democracy, howsoever laudable it might be, must subject itself to the overriding credo of "*Vasudhaika Kutumbam*", the concept of One World. When applied to globalisation, the component of "recognition of divinity in every man and woman" would mean that all human beings irrespective of their caste, creed, race and nationality deserve to be and become rightful claimants of the benefits of globalisation. The second component, *viz.*, "everybody's inherent right to liberation or *moksha*" denotes that all the countries have a right to work out their own ways and means of participating in the globalisation process. The overriding factor of *Vasudhaika Kutumbam*, however, underscores the supremacy of Cosmos and enjoins that the *modus operandi* of globalisation as well as sharing its gains should not only be at the cost of the interests of others, but should also be such that the economic growth and social welfare of the mankind as a whole is as high as possible.

Unleashing India's potential in the context of examining India's role in the globalisation process, should be aimed at humanising globalisation through value based Spiritual Democracy so that its process is humanistic and sharing of its gains is just and equitable. Is it not significant that the concept of Spiritual Democracy has been introduced by an Indian, Swami Vivekananda at the equally significant First World Parliament of Religions held in Chicago in September 1893? Is it not equally significant that a celebrated historian like Arnold Toynbee stated, "Modern materialistic civilization which is a chapter which had a Western beginning, will have to have an Indian end if it is not to end in the destruction of mankind"? Finally, it may not be out of place to note that A.L. Basham, an Australian scholar, after an in-depth study of Indian civilization, came to the conclusion that "the most striking feature of ancient Indian civilization is its humanity". Not surprisingly he gave title to his research study as 'The Wonder that was India.'

■ Indian Insights, Experiences and Practices

J.N. Tata, the pioneer of Iron and Steel industry in India, wrote a letter to Swami Vivekananda in 1918 in which he mentioned: "I very much recall at this moment your views on the growth of ascetic spirit in India, and the duty of not destroying, but of diverting into useful channels. It seems to me that no better use can be made of the ascetic spirit than establishment of monasteries or residential halls for men dominated by this spirit where they should live with ordinary decency and devote their lives to the cultivation of sciences natural and humanistic......

"If such a crusade were undertaken by a competent leader, it would greatly help a citizen, science and the good name of our country."

The Mother's Ministry of Management at Sri Aurobindo Ashram, Pondicherry, comes perhaps nearest to implementing Spiritual Democracy at an institutional level "Management is harmonizing men, material and methods towards the fulfillment of goals leading to human development social benefit and global welfare. However, MAN remains the basic factor in any field of human endeavour – it may be home, hospital, business, industry or any other profit/non-profit socio-economic organisation. By MAN we do not mean here only a lump of bones and flesh, nor an 'amalgam' of hands, feet and physical frame, but a 'conscious creature' designed by a Divine Craftsman. He has a spirit and a soul. Management of man, therefore, should not aim at mere regulation and control of his outer appearance but it should be developing his inner consciousness, his soul and his divinity". (Sri Aurobindo Society, Pondicherry, The Mother's Ministry of Management, 1990).

In recent times Indian industry has realized the role of values in an organisation as a means of increasing employee commitment and productivity. Since '90s, when India has joined the globalization process, such efforts at integrating values with organisation culture are being strengthened for enhancing their competitiveness at international level. Infosys, for instance, believes in "Powered by Intellect, Driven by Values". Narayana Murthy, while stepping down as its Chairman last year, stated that "Infosys is not a company selling software, but a global corporation, with an enduring value system". Kumara Mangalam Birla feels that "The Birla group is currently facing *vis-à-vis* its globalization process five major challenges.... The fifth of these challenges involves making one's globalization character successful and sustainable. What bonds us are our values- integrity, speed, seamlessness, commitment and passion. We expect these values to define the character of our corporation,...."

In the context of escalating competitive pressures, which is a hallmark of globalization, ITC Ltd., believes that "The enlargement of enterprise potential (therefore) requires Vision, Values and Vitality to be continuously recharged through practice and insight, revalidated for relevance and tested for appropriateness to the evolving competitive context." (ITC Chairman's Speech at its 95th Annual General Meeting, 2006)

In the milieu of Mergers and Acquisitions (M&A), which also has become another important hallmark of globalization, human values as a means of creating the required equation in human interactions have become significant. Ratan

Tata, for instance, has recently stated (*vis-à-vis* Tata-Corus M&A) that Tata's first evaluated a company's value system before acquiring or merging with it "as values and human chemistry are very important to us".

Quoting the Global Forum of Spiritual Leaders and Parliamentarians held in Kremlin, the then USSR, in March 1990 would perhaps be an appropriate conclusion to this discussion: "A return to values is inescapable if we do not wish to hand over a dead stone to our children rather than a live planet". The role of India in this process of return to values by the mankind can hardly be exaggerated.

Endnotes

Select Reflections for Introspection

1. **Manmohan Singh,** Prime Minister of India: We have a global economy of sorts, but it is not supported by a global quality.

2. **John F. Kennedy:** If a free society cannot help the many who are poor, it cannot save the few who are rich.

3. **Thay (Thich Nhat Hanh, Zen Master):** Development is like a wild horse that we are riding, over which we have lost control.

4. **Amartya Sen:** Advocates a people centered rather than growth centered approach to development.

5. **Ed Cohen, (2007):** Across the globe, those who have the leadership characteristics, business acumen, world view, people and business leadership skills to be successful and who are willing to take these risks will become more and more marketable.

6. **Global Forum of Spiritual Leaders and Parliamentarians,** Kremlin, USSR, March 1990 A return to values is inescapable if we do not wish to handover a dead stone to our children rather than a live planet.

7. **Symbiosis between Science and Spirit:** Karan Singh in *The Times of India,* The Best of Speaking Tree: 2004-2006: Spirituality transcends barriers of race, religion, creed and nationality. Seers of all great faiths have sought to describe what is essentially an indescribable experience, whether it is the Beatific Vision of the Christians, the Bodhichitta of Buddhists, the *Noor-e-Ilahi* of Muslim's , the Ek Omkar of the Sikh Guru's or the Self Realization of the Hindus. Clearly, these are states of higher consciousness which are the heritage of the entire human race. This flows from the persistent tradition of the light that aluminates the universe – that of consciousness itself. It is awareness of this light in all human beings that alone can become the corner stone of a harmonious global society. What is needed is a symbiosis between the inner and the outdoor, the quietist and the activists, and in the broader dimension between science and spirituality.

8. **Sri Ravi Shankar:** 'It is spirituality from Puja Room to Board Room', *The Times of India*, guest editor, Dec. 2006: Make spirituality an attitude and not just a practice !

   A practice is always bound by time but an attitude gets woven into that time. A practice is limited to occasion and to time and has a time bound impact which wears off after a while and has to be revived. But an attitude gets woven into yourself.

❑❑❑

EPILOGUE Back to Self

Epilogue:
Back to Self

> *Everybody can be great because anybody can serve. You don't have to have a college degree to serve. You don't have to make your subject and verb agree to serve. You only need a heart full of grace. A soul generated by love.*
>
> — **Martin Luther King, Jr.**

■ Revival of Confucius (March 2009): Its Significance

In March 2009, there has been a news item, not conspicuous by any means – to the affect that Confucius, the ancient Chinese Philosopher had been revived China. He had been denounced just a few decades ago as a feudal thinker because of his emphasis on harmony and respect of social hierarchy which conflicted with the Marxist ideology of 'Progress through Conflict'. Although, the information is about reviving a particular set of thoughts and actions, its implications are far reaching and deserve closer attention, in the context of humanising mankind.

The origin of the issue of harmony *vs.* conflict, co-operation *vs.* competition, peace *vs.* war goes back to the origin of human beings. As discussed till recently it was thought that it was the violence and beastliness which dominated the human thinking and action at its earliest stage. Recent understanding has questioned the thesis and come out to show that it is the co-operative spirit and caring and sharing which was the pre-dominant factor in human behaviour. The theory of cooperative man is now widely accepted.

The conflict, both within and outside of the good and bad, virtue and vice, white and black has had been existing together right from the being of social behaviour of human beings. That violence is within us is noted by even a humanist like Mother Teresa and widely proved empirically also. The correction factor in such a situation becomes the environment, beginning from mother and family. That inner divinity is within us is equally accepted and widely shared by all religions and faith. It is said that to see the Godly behaviour, one has just to observe, the infants being on their own for a certain amount of time. The factor which veers the human beings from the innocence and godliness is gain the environment.

The human history bears testimony to these inner and outer turmoil's in dependent of place and time. Such turmoil's are manifested at economic, political, social and ideological levels. Of late however, there has been rethinking that the dichotomies between different 'ism's' is reducing.

It was Francis Fukuyama, of John Hopkins University, USA who came out in his classic work, 'The End of History and The Last Man (1992)' with the argument that the progression of human history as a struggle between ideologies is largely at an end. He adds that, after the end of the 'cold war' and the fall of the Berlin Wall, in 1989, the world is settling on liberal democracy. "What we may be witnessing is not just end of the cold war, or the passing of a particular period of post-war, but the end of history as such.........that is the end point of mankind's ideological evolution and the universalisation of western liberal democracy as the final form of human government". It is in this context, that the revival of Confucius is to be understood.

Confucius, King Fu-Tzu as the title goes was belonging to the elite class and believed in the intrinsic goodness of humans and their inclination towards living in harmony. In spite of this background, and the fact that China stands for Communism-perhaps the only country which can be called communist now a days – and strong in its ideological moorings and firmness did think fit enough to revive 'Confucianism' is a subtle but significant pointer to inter-ideological co existence.

Ideological reconciliation implied by Francis Fukuyama also denotes greater understanding and acceptance of others viewpoints at ideological level. The openness in human thinking and attitudes, a logical corollary is the basic premise of the book.

Peter Berger, an American sociologist, known for his work *The Social Construction of Reality: A Treatise in the Sociology of Knowledge* , argues that the key feature of the 20th Century has been growing acceptance that self realisation of the individual is a greater goal than loyalty to any group like the family, religion, , race, ruling dynasty or nation.

Both Democracy and Capitalism are about empowering individuals or groups. Democracy appears to do the needful for individual empowerment. It is not evident however that Capitalism and Markets are also about empowering the individuals over groups. Berger on the other hand underscores the empowerment of the individual and recognition that individual self realisation is the most important of goals. This view point is again in consonance with 'Confucianism' and the premise of the book.

Raine Eisler, Social Scientist analyses the evolution of culture and ideas over 10,000 years of human history and points out that two opposing ideas of Social Organisation have contended, with each other at various times. One is the idea of partnerships and equality , principally among the two sexes. Whenever this model has prevailed there has been greater peace and an effervescence of creativity. The other idea, more prevalent, is domination by hierarchy's with a single leader invariably male at the top. The dominator model she explains is intolerant of opposition. Eisler believes, that western civilization is essentially that of dominator model. This model produces results but not in all context. When problems are systemic, when there are many interacting forces with reinforcing and balancing amongst them, when many actors must collaborate to understand the system of which they are all a part and co-operate in its improvement partnerships are necessary.

The spirit of co-operation and harmony are basic to 'Confucianism'. *Spandan* approach is also based upon the spirit of co-operation between and among the individual, groups and the orgnanisations.

The present day context, when institutions are becoming organic, world has become a global village and where the organisational hierarchies have become of more an exception than rule, and teamwork has replaced individual leadership, the importance of model of partnership can hardly be exaggerated.

■ Consciousness: The Crux of Remaking Ourselves

Mashubi Rochell, an American Spiritual Counsellor discusses the importance of consciousness in human development in the thoughtful article, 'Healing Despair (2008)'. Mashubi states, "The thesis of the article is that today's world is reaching a crisis point and the way out is through consciousness. The root of the world's problems has to do with our consciousness. It started with where our collective consciousness has been. Humanity has been involved in developing our individuality and in experiencing the world of physical reality without much attention to the larger whole of which we are a part. This was a necessary step in our evolution, but now times have changed..... We have chosen to use energy resources that are finite and cause pollution......All of these challenges we now face started with a consciousness that had forgotten our essential connection to the larger whole of life. We are divine beings that entered into physical reality in order to learn, and now at this crucial time in the evolution of humanity, we are beginning to learn how to reconnect with ourselves, with each other and with the earth. We are beginning to learn that our thoughts create our reality and that we think and feel matters as much as what we do. One of the great spiritual truths shared with us by all spiritual teachers and religions is that we are all connected. We are a part of God, who lives within us."

Our understanding of the importance of consciousness of self and the universe can be summed up by quoting authorities from two different faiths. Swami Nityaswarupananda: observes that "The universe has not existence independent of the Self, what we see is only the projection of the mind. The moment we bring about a change in our consciousness the universe changes for us. The Self is the only real substance. Existence its very nature" Daisaku Ikeda states that "We need to awaken to a common consciousness of all being inhabitants of Earth. This consciousness is not be found on a computer screen. It lies in our hearts, in our ability to share the pain of our fellow human beings".

■ In Conclusion

It may be recalled that the basic tenet of *Spandan* inner divinity of human beings by human being themselves for re-inventing themselves as human beings. The behavioural manifestation of innate divinity has been taken as the basic goodness of a human being. When applied to a particular individual it would mean that he is good basically, believes that other are basically good and accordingly weaves his sentiments interactions and activities with others. The Position, Projection and Perception under this situation are expected to have congruence between and among themselves. Its antecedent is the interplay of Head, Heart and perhaps soul at three planes of human personality, namely *viz.*, *Manasa* (Consciousness), *Vacha* (saying – communication), and *Karmanye* (doings – action). When applied to symbolizes the process of humanising. The first step is to h or remake humanise or remake himself, in terms of appropriate attitudes and values, where he becomes the subject predicate and object, all rolled in one. This self humanising is to take place at individual, professional and organsiational levels. The second step is facilitate others where he becomes subject and verb (catalyst) and the others become object (focal persons).

Beyond management of organisations, the concepts of innate divinity and basic goodness applies to human beings, at the levels of society, nation, the world and the universe. The crux of the issue at that point is consciousness – the universal consciousness being the ultimatum.

Endnotes

1. **S. Radhakrishnan,** Indian Philosopher and former President of India: There is so much of inequality, so much of injustice in this world. It is the human individual who has to realize that God is the spark in him.

2. **Confucius:** If there be righteousness in the Heart, there will be beauty in the Character. If there be Beauty in the Character there will be Harmony in the Home. If there be Harmony in the Home there will be order in the Nation. If there be order in the Nation, there will be peace in the World.

3. **On the Universe:**

   Albert Einstein: "Two things are infinite; the universe and human stupidity; and I am not sure about the universe". "The most incomprehensible thing about the universe is that is comprehensive".

   J.B.S. Haldayne: The Universe is not than we imagine, it is queerer than we can imagine.

4. **Dr. Edgar Mitchell,** Apollo 14 astronaut, 1971: In his introduction to the 'Cosmic Detective' by Mani Bhaumik, (2008), Mitchell states as follows: While returning to Earth, after landing on the Moon in January, 1971, he felt the epiphany that was his experience of 'Universal Oneness' as I was looking at the distant oasis of Earth against the velvety darkness of space, punctuated by stars and galaxies, normally only viewed through earthbound telescopes.

5. **Daisaku Ikeda:** We need to awaken to a common consciousness of all being inhabitants of Earth. This consciousness is not to be found on a computer screen. It lies in our hearts, in our ability to share the pain of our fellow human beings.

❑❑❑

APPENDICES

Appendix to Chapter 8:
Spandan Workshops at Delta Information Services, Chandigarh, 2007

Appendix to Chapter 16:
Success Stories of Weavers, Jaipur Rugs Company, Jaipur

Appendix to Chapter 8: *Spandan* Workshops at Delta Information Services, Chandigarh, 2007

The *Spandan* Workshops are organized as part of the process of integrating values with work ethic and anchored to the Misssion Statement of the organisation. The process takes around an year to complete one cycle of the process with *Spandan* as External Facilitator. After the completion of one cycle, the organisation is expected to continue the process with the Core Group assuming the role of Internal Facilitator.

With a view to have 'a feel' of how the workshops are conducted with experiential learning as its anchor in the presence of Facilitator from *Spandan*, the Minutes and Proceedings of the Workshops held in an organisation spreading over three days are reproduced. These workshops were organised by the Delta Services (I) Ltd., Chandigarh on three days, May 25-27, 2007 in Chandigarh. The eight participants in the workshops were the Managing Director and seven Departmental Heads constituting the Core Group. The objective of the Core Group – following the process as enunciated in the previous section – was to be the executive arm for introducing the management of change in the Company through Diagnosis, Discovery and Development. After the completion of the first cycle of inculcation of values in the Company with *Spandan* as Facilitator, the Core Group would ensure that the process continues on an ongoing basis.

Delta *Spandan* Workshop on Human Values – Venue: IDS Conference Room, Mohali Date/s: 25th–26th–27th May'07

Day 1

The session opened with Round 0, which was a warm up session and participants were asked to introduce the Company. The main points that were mentioned were:

- The areas of operation of the company
- The age of the company
- The leader of the company

There were further discussions on definition of a leader and the tone of the workshop was set on the aspect of Leadership, *i.e.*, Transforming Passion to Professionalism.

■ Round 1

We next proceeded to Round 1, the Diagnosis step of the 3-D Approach. The output of the Diagnosis was the Objective statement of Delta

Task: Individual → Small Group → Large Group

Focus: State the Primary Objective of the Organisation.

Once each member penned down his/her thoughts, 4 groups were formulated of 3-4 members each and they were assigned the task to collectively come up with the Primary Objective Statement for the Organisation. And finally 4 members (one from each group) joined to come up with the Common 'Primary Objective' Statement of the Organisation, as stated below:

■ To be amongst the Top 5 Quality Education and Training Providers Nationally

- Ensuring Long Term Profitability and Growth
- Contributing to the Success of Individuals and Organisations
- Excelling in Our Corporate Social Responsibilities and
- Continuously Exploring and Integrating New Opportunities and Avenues.

■ 4 Aspects of Group Dynamics were also Ascertained

- The thoughts of Individuals and Group may not necessarily be the same; they may be similar

- They should be similar
- Quality of Output is increased in a group owing to greater functional wavelength.
- Every member in a group may not be equally participating. The influencer – who may be a person of higher authority or may otherwise have influence on the group, mostly majorly contributes to the decision.

Round 2

We next moved to Round 2, the Discovery round.

Task: Individual

Focus: To what extent has Delta achieved the particular objective.

Here, all members were asked to give a ranking on a scale of 1-10 (1 being lowest and 10 being highest). The members were asked to rank on the following 3 parameters:

- Company as a whole
- Division/Centres
- Self

Name	Company	Division	Self
JB	7		
AK	8		
BD	7		
AJ	6		
IV	6		
MJ	2		
AD	6		
PM	4		
PR	4		
SK	7		
MD	8		
SJK	5		
VC	6		
RS	6		

However, assessment in the group was done only on the Company's ranking.

Summary	Company	Div.	Self
Mean	6.25		
#NOP's	13		
Range	2 to 8		
#NOP's	#1 #2		
Less than 5	3		

The following observations were made:

- □ A high variance in the responses as the range varied from 2 to 8
  - 1 person gave a ranking of 2
  - 2 persons gave a ranking of 8
- □ 3 members gave a ranking of less than 5
  - 1 person gave a ranking of 2
  - 2 persons gave a ranking of 4
- □ The mean came out to be 6.25, which was very close to the rank (6) assigned by the common leader, Renu. This meant that the perception of the leader and other's were similar.

There were further arguments on possible reasons of such an extreme range, specially why some member gave such a low ranking… 3 such possible reasons were identified:

- □ The member may be unaware
- □ The member may be aware but not satisfied
- □ The expectations are high and hence the ranking low, *viz.*, our assessment is a function of our own bench mark. People who rank low have a significant role to play.

■ Round 3

We further moved to Round 3, the Development round.

Task: Small Group

Focus: Why the company ranks 6? Why not beyond 6?

The groups were asked to give top 3 reasons as to Why the company ranks 6? Why not beyond 6?

■ Group A

- ☐ Brand building
- ☐ New avenues – Faster Decision
- ☐ Proper selection – new joinees, some benchmark

■ Group B

- ☐ Professionalism – HR process
- ☐ Restricted avenues
- ☐ Non-conformance to systems
  - Customer Intake
  - Delivery

■ Group C

- ☐ Exploring avenues beyond current set up
- ☐ Top strategy for diversification and Zero Defect execution
- ☐ Effective communication and Manpower planning (new and current set up)

■ Group D

- ☐ Exploring new ventures
- ☐ Lack of community Projects (Brand)
- ☐ High attrition
- ☐ Lack of World Class infra

After each group shared their views, 4 major reasons that were identified with a consensus were:

1. Delta is not established as Brand
2. Redefine the HR policies
3. Infrastructure – "Bench Trending should be there"
4. Conformance to systems

It was further ascertained that if something is not done, it is either because of:

- ☐ Inability
- ☐ Unwillingness or
- ☐ Unawareness (Awareness is "Acceptance of Ignorance")

Keeping this in view, the statements were modified to

1. Our Inability to build Delta as a Brand
2. Our unawareness of frequently reviewing the HR policies as per the changing Industry environment
3. Our inability to build a World Class infrastructure
4. Our unawareness of currently setup systems and processes

Every one was further asked to vote whether the areas in which the company lacked were controllable or uncontrollable, to which each one said that all the factors are controllable.

The next question was to what extent did the recognized weaknesses fall in the "people or non-people responsibility dimension"

It was ascertained with consensus that HR and Systems, are pre-dominantly 'people responsibility', rest was left open.

■ Round 4

Task: Individual

Focus: Focal Person Activity

Renu, being the common leader of the workgroup was identified as the focal person.

Each member was asked to list 3 strengths of the focal person, and later 3 improvement areas

The strengths which listed in the consolidated top 3 were;

- ☐ Dedication (#3)
- ☐ Hardworking (#3)
- ☐ Good at Communication (#3)

and further, strengths which had a mention twice were

- ☐ Familiarity with systems
- ☐ Good Listener
- ☐ Self-Disciplined
- ☐ Analytical approach

The areas of improvement identified were

- ☐ Listening Skills
- ☐ Spending time with 'team members' at centers

One more area of improvement was listed by Renu – Impatient

At the end of Day-1, some more conclusions were drawn

- ☐ Create, Operate and improve – the 3-D approach
- ☐ A system is as good or as bad as its people
- ☐ If one has to improve, we need to have a 360° feedback
- ☐ Introspection without feedback is of no use and similarly feedback without introspection is of no use

With this the 1st day concluded; everyone was given an assignment to come up with "Hallmark of a Professional" the next day.

Day 2

■ Round 5

Task: Large Group

Focus: Share the Hallmarks of a Professional

The session on day 2 began with discussion on "Hallmarks of a Professional",

Major outcomes of the discussion were; a Professional is one who

- ☐ Balances his/her personal life and Professional life
- ☐ Is good at team management
- ☐ Exhibits Self Control

Regarding Self control ↔ Good Decision making
(If too high, becomes doormat) emotional detachment

- ☐ An approach of balance of Emotional Detachment and Professional attachment while doing the job
- ☐ Admirable mix of Science and Art, "Personally Impersonal Impersonally Personal"
- ☐ To define who is a professional – The KSA approach can also be taken as a crutch
  - 1 person gave a ranking of 2
  - K – knowledge (what)
  - S – skills (how)
  - A – attitude (why) Must be aware ~ strong belief ~ should be the inner strength

The only way to describe a professional is "ATTITUDES"

■ Round 6

Task: Individual

Focus: To rank the following:

6.1 How good is my company?

6.2 How good are the people in my company?

6.3 How good is my boss as a boss?

6.4 How good is the top man?

6.5 How good am I myself?

The people ranked as

Name	6.1	6.2	6.3	6.4	6.5
BD	6	4	7	8	8
AK	7	7	9	8	8
JB	6	5	8	9	7
PR	9	7	9	9	8
MJ	5	5	5	5	5
PM	7	7	8	8	7
AD	8	8	9	10	8
IV	7	7	6	9	6
ML	7	6	7	8	6
SK	5	6	8	8	7
AJ	4	8	6	8	6
VC	4	6	6	8	5
SJK	7	7	7	7	7
RS	7	7	9	9	7

The following table was obtained:

Item no.	Mean	Range		Above or below 5	
		Min	Max	^{3} 5	< 5
6.1	6.35	4 (#2)	9 (#1)	86%	14%
6.2	6.42	4 (#1)	8 (#2)	93%	7%
6.3	7.42	5 (#1)	9 (#4)	100%	0
6.4	8.14	5 (#1)	10 (#1)	100%	0
6.5	6.78	5 (#2)	8 (#4)	100%	0

Some interesting observations were made:

- "Co. & people rating is similar" (± 0.5): The mean for Q. No. 6.1 & 6.2 came out to be 6.3 & 6.4 respectively, which further emphasized the fact that a company is as good or as bad as its people.
- Huge gap between ratings for Q. No. 6.4, (*i.e.*, 8.14) & Q. No. 6.2, (*i.e.*, 6.42); Top Boss is the role model
- Scope of improvement for MD: 8.14-6.35
- Focus on "How good am I myself"; 6.78 is higher than 6.42 (I'm okay – you are not okay phenomenon is visible)
- In a professional environment, goodness of people was taken to be on the factors of
  - Dedication to do the job
  - Ability and willingness

Another question that was put across was to rank "own" & "Others" in the company on a 5-point scale of

- Wholly Good
- Basically Good
- Cannot say / ZERO
- Basically Bad
- Wholly Bad

It was pretty interesting to note that all 14 ranked 'own' as well as 'others' in the company as "basically good". It was derived that "behaviour is a function of individual and situation". The impact of 'situation' cannot be eliminated.

$$B = f(i, s)$$

Why not Wholly Good?

- There is a scope for improvement.
- Not "perfection" achieved.
- The only thing that interferes with my learning is my education.
- Not a "culture"/"value" – definition of learning involves unlearning.

Why we should not think of 'Basically Bad'?

- Work is given – work is not done.
- Negative feeling comes in mind/ what prevented him from doing the job.
- Sees no scope of improvement – (I'm ok – you're not ok syndrome).

■ Round 7

Task: Small Group

Focus: Which 5 values, out of the list of 44, if adopted by the company will enhance 'dedication to duty' of the employees? (the motto was strengthening strengths and weakening weaknesses)

The top 5 listed by the groups were:

- Support (3 tally points)
- Fairness (3 tally points)
- Employee Needs (3 tally points)
- Trusting Other's (3 tally points)
- Freedom (2 tally points)

and One more value of 'Conviction' was added from the values listed by the Common Leader.

Task: Small Group

Focus: How to operationalize each of the values?

The following 3 factors had to be addressed:

- Definition of the value
- What are they?
- How can they be operationalised?

1. Freedom:
   (*a*) Clear Communication
   (*b*) Well defined Roles and Tasks
   (*c*) Documented Norms and Values
   (*d*) Extent of financial implication/Finance availability
   (*e*) Timeframe to execute
2. Fairness:
   (*a*) Clear and Transparent Communication – Policy & JDS, RTOPS
   (*b*) Similar problems of different employees be dealt in similar fashion
3. Conviction:
   (*a*) Dedication
   (*b*) Flexible role handling/additional responsibility in different roles

4. Support:
   (*a*) Training for better understanding
   (*b*) Listening to ideas
   (*c*) Rewards
   (*d*) Authority and decision
5. Trusting Others:
   (*a*) Educate first/suggest
6. Employee Needs: Define – Expectations from Job and Organisation
   (*a*) Clear communication – 'HR' recruitment, induction
   (*b*) Regular feed back session/ open house
   (*c*) Personal reviews
   (*d*) Listening sessions – understanding the needs

It was further added that this value may be rephrased to 'Employee Needs and Expectations'

■ Round 8

Task: Individual

Focus: Pick one Value and create the Plan of Action for next 2-3 months

The outcome was

- ☐ Employee needs was chosen by 4 individuals
- ☐ Support by 3
- ☐ Freedom by 3
- ☐ Trusting others by 2
- ☐ Conviction by 1
- ☐ Fairness by 1

For the presentations, an observation group was formulated consisting of Poonam, Jitender and Vikas on the criterion of:

- ☐ Tenure and position within the company
- ☐ Transparency
- ☐ Newest person in the organisation

2 members, Priti and Simran, were nominated to present the plans on their chosen value. Priti had chosen Employee needs and Simran had chosen Support. Further presentations and discussions on the 2 values helped in establishing

Steps to be taken to strengthen the value of 'Employee needs':

1. Formulation of an HR Cell
2. Formulation of work group to work on redefining the HR policy manual
   (*a*) Psychometric test to be included in Selection process
3. Conduct of attitude survey thru Individual Effectiveness Feedback Survey
4. 360° Feedback mechanism to be built
   (*a*) Immediate supervisor
   (*b*) Colleagues
5. Open house sessions
6. External body to be involved in employee satisfaction survey
7. Concept of a 'mentor'

Steps to be taken to strengthen the value of Support needs:

1. Documents to be created on Sales and Delivery and provided across all locations
2. Trainings to be held
3. Recruitment: Focus on intake of employee; KSA of new joinee
4. Listening to new team members

■ Round 9

Task: Individual

Focus: Focal Person Activity

Abhay was selected as the Focal person.

Again everyone was asked to list 3 strengths and 3 areas of improvement. Major strengths that came to light were:

■ 3 Major Strengths

Good Comm. Skills (#14)

Presentation Skills (#4)

Confidence (#2)

■ 3 Major Areas of Improvement

Stays in area of concern (#5)

Time Management (#4)

Switching Ability (Bandwidth) (#2)

Informal touch with Team members (#1)

■ Johari's Window

Any leader has to do 2 functions:

Task function (Objective is there → Achieve it)

Social Emotional function (Task is there → Achieve Task as well as take care of 'people')

Do well: The task function; task orientation

Do well willingly: Social Emotional function; achieve task as well as take care of people

Seldom a person is equally effective on both the functions… some are temperamentally good at 1 and others at 2.. we need to try and balance 'both'

Ratings were done for Abhay:

Name	Task Function	Social-Emotional Function
BD	6	4
VC	6	4
JB	4	6
PR	4	6
AD	8	2
IV	7	3
SK	6	4
AK	6	4
SK	6	4
RS	7	3

■ Round 10

The session on day 2 concluded with Round 10

Task: Individual

Focus: Definition of Personality

Personality was identified as an important dimension of the 'individual' in the equation 'Behaviour is a function of individual and situation'. Personality–4 components:

Personality	Physiological (Body)	Cognitive (Knowledge)	Emotional	Conation (Action)
Real Self-perception Perception by Others				

Comments on the quote "I think, therefore I am; I am, therefore I think" were invited and everyone was asked to give some thought to the questions

- Who am I?
- What am I?

The responses were very interesting varying from someone saying she's a mother, daughter, computer professional and Jitender's response, "I am a bachelor" was the prizewinner.

Dr. Rao shared that 'Who Am I?' is 'Relational' whereas 'What am I?' is independent of atmosphere/cosmos

And with this, day 2 came to a close.

Day 3

Round 11

Day 3 began with discussions on "I am, what I am"

Everyone was asked to share what they understood of this quotation.

1. What does it mean?
2. How is it relevant to me as a 'Role Holder'?

Various viewpoints were shared, *viz.*,

- My strengths and weaknesses
- Accept myself as I am (Not pretending to be what I'm)
- I am satisfied with what I am
- Each one is responsible for his/her response

Process that was identified thru discussion was

Step 1 – Diagnosis: Develop a mechanism to understand who is what?

Step 2 – Identify gaps between self-perception and that of boss and work towards reducing it.

What are the different types of ramifications of "I am what I am"

- Real abilities
- The abilities that I think I have
- Abilities my boss thinks I have
- Abilities I think my boss thinks I have

It was also discussed that in our perception of self, mostly the strengths are magnified and we are unaware of our weaknesses. The other aspect is that of 'Hanuman' ~ unaware of own strength. In such a situation, inventory of ability is there, it is upon the leader to educate the member.

■ Round 12

Next was the incidence method.

Here the task was to have an open discussion on any live incident:

Amitoz discussed a Case Study, a live incident from where some points were identified, where one could relate to Human Values.

The incident was discussed and the following learning's came out based on the incident.

1. What matters is the role relation.
2. "Whose baby is it", also matters?
3. How important is the issue?
4. What is the worth to follow it – Cost benefit Analysis?
5. What are the long term and short term solutions?
6. Controllability/do we have the authority.
7. Empathetic Listening.

It was established that asking the right kind of question solves half the problem.

■ Round 13

Task: Individual

Focus: Value Diagnosis – A comparative Analysis

Here the different values, which were identified, were compared

- Delta Values, *i.e.*, the pre-workshop values.
- The values that were deduced in Round 7 (6 values after 3 round of analysis).
- The values entered by the employees in the reference sheet.

On comparing, it was observed that the thinking of the company remains same to an extent of 50%. The task further assigned was whether the 9 identified values, *viz.*,

- Conviction
- Creativity
- Competition
- Discipline
- Devotion to duty
- Employee Performance (present)
- Commitment
- Profits

were good enough as values of the Company. the parameter identified here was whether the set of values catered to all the stake holders, *viz.*, company, customer, Employee and stake holder. Following comparison was drawn:

Value	Company	Customer	Employee	Stake Holders
Conviction			✓	
Creativity	✓		✓	
Competition			✓	
Discipline			✓	
Devotion to duty			✓	
Employee Performance (present)	✓		✓	
Commitment			✓	
Profits	✓			✓
Customer Orientation		✓		

The deduction was that the mix isn't good enough as the major inclination is towards the 'employees', whereas it should be balanced. Hence, the Values may have to be re-visited

■ Round 14

Task: Small Group

Focus: To identify 5 values from the Management cum Professional's point of view – Which 5 values if made part of work ethics, will motivate you to give the best to the company?

The values finally identified were:

- □ Employee needs
- □ Customer orientation
- □ Conviction
- □ Prosperity
- □ Creativity

■ Round 15

Task: Small Group

Focus: Values for the Prospective Professionals: The task was to identify any 5 values, with the assumption that these may be incorporated as a part of course curriculum or voluntary courses to make the students Industry ready.

Groups were made and the discussion was done. The differentiator from the previous rounds was that only 2 values could be taken from the listed 44 values and 3 had to be original in idea.

Values Identified	Tally Points
Self-Discipline	#3
Flexibility	#2
Positive Attitude	#2
Ethic Moral Values	#2

The outcome of the entire deliberations and discussions was that we need to incorporate 2 types of trainings in the curriculum:-

■ Reality Orientation

- □ Adapativeness (willing/able/aware)
- □ Culture

■ Personality Development

- □ Positive attitude
- □ Open mindedness and Bright
- □ Communication and soft skills (Inter-personal Skills)
- □ Ethic moral soundness(inner strength ~ conviction)

■ Round 16

The discussion was on *Spandan*, its concept, how it evolved and how it is managing to help people by its concept of maternalistic management.

- □ Knowing one's own limitations.
- □ Knowingly not doing anything wrong.
- □ Can I be a little 'less' perfect – something more; something different; something better.

The maternalisitic management and disciplinary management of mother and father were discussed. Do I know the need of the team members without 'communication'? Have ESP – Extra Sensory Perception.

■ Round 17

Task: Individual

Focus: Industry expectations – identify values for prospective professionals. Values which majorly came across were:

- □ Containment of Greed
- □ Respect for others (leading by example)

■ Round 18

Task: Individual

Focus: Focal Person Activity

Inder was selected as the Focal person.

Again everyone was asked to list 3 strengths and 3 areas of improvement. Major strengths that came to light were:

■ 3 Major Strengths

Strong systems knowledge (#13)

Helpful (#4)

Data analytical skills

■ 3 Major Areas of Improvement

Reflection on Peers

Communication skills

Hasty decision maker

With this we approached the close of the workshop Round Zee, where the focus, was pay off.

Task was to identify individually

1. What is it that I take as an area of improvement for myself?
2. What is that I carry for my unit?

Name	My Improvement	Div.
JB	3-D as an attitude	Strengthen the strength; weaken the weakness
IV	Think – say – do	
PM	Time mgmt. and allocation	Doc. of Spandan
AK	3-D as an attitude	3-D for futurz analysis
MJ	Projection to be strengthened	3-D for Sales, Education Delivery, IC cell
AD	Focus from self to SELF	
PR	Creativity – identify opportunities	2nd tier, *i.e.*, HOC's in MT/NIIT – maintain monthly calendar
ML	3-D for self and others	3-D f/b system with Biz. Team
BD	Focal person activity	2nd tier in MT/NIIT – maintain monthly calendar
SJK	3-P approach as an attitude	Training for Sales team, Creation of Sales docket
RS	3-D culture	
AJ	Constant introspection – work on f/b	3-D for Service Delivery
SK	Maternalistic approach	

With this, the *Spandan* workshop came to an end.

As can be noted the above Minutes and Proceedings of the three day *Spandan* Workshops held at Delta is a veritable mine throwing several insights, raising several issues and offering leads for future action. This task will be undertaken in the next chapter.

With the understanding gained of the model of the 3-D Process and its dynamics as demonstrated during the three days of workshops at the Delta Information Services, Chandigarh, we would like to have, in the next chapter insights in its rationale and '*modus operandi*'.

Appendix to Chapter 16: Success Stories of Weavers, Jaipur Rugs Company, Jaipur

■ I can be Like You!

Name: Rekha Rathore

Occupation: Master Trainer for carpet weaving

Rekha is aged 19 years and hails from a very poor family residing in Pailiya (Churu). She belongs to the Rajput community, a community in which girls are forbidden access to education, health or travelling. She is survived by her father, mother, two brothers and a younger sister. While her father has migrated to Jaipur in search of a better pay, Rekha being the eldest of the children was allowed to complete her schooling till eighth standard. Her village-Pailiya in Churu does not have secondary, senior secondary schools or health facilities available. For classes after eighth standard, students in this village need to travel to the main district Ratangarh which is around 10-15 kms away from this village. The transportation facilities are also very minimal. If anyone needs to travel from Pailiya to Ratangarh, they need to catch up with city buses that have very odd timings of arrival and departure. It has been witnessed that a majority of drunk labours travel in such buses from nearby villages that makes it uncomfortable for any female candidate to travel.

This was a sad reason because of which Rekha couldn't convince her parents to send her to senior secondary school so that she could at least finish her schooling. The result was obvious. She was forced to leave the dream of being a literate lady. "Yaha par ladkiyo ko padaya nahi jaata hai. Kash mere bas mein hota toh mein aap jaisi banjati" (Here females are not allowed to pursue education. I wish if I had the powers to become like you!), Rekha said when one of our team members visited her home.

Her father is currently working as an inventory care taker for a plywood firm in Jaipur. Earlier, he was working in a garment store in Surat where he earned just about Rs. 5000 pm and was the only earning member in the family. Staying away from home and working in an unhealthy environment, he gradually developed infection in his lungs because of which he was bed ridden for at least three years. Some small savings in her father's account could provide their groceries. Rekha was just 15 then and looking at their financial conditions, she started to seek work. Sewing and stitching caught her attention. Her aunt came forward to help her find clients from nearby villages. She started sewing for her aunt's friends and known relatives. Travelling alone to receive orders and deliver, however, was very difficult. At first, her parents and siblings didn't agree to send her elsewhere. For some days she lied to her parents that she is visiting her neighborhood friends and would smartly vanish with no traces behind to her client's places in search of better orders. "Jab meine pehli baar us mahine Rs. 200 kamaye, muje andaar se khushi bhi hui aur dar laga. Khushi isiliye hui ki main ab kamao ho gayi aur dar isiliye kyuki meine jhoot bola tha," said Rekha. (For the first month when I earned Rs. 200 I was very overwhelmed and at the same time, a fear crept my mind. I was happy because I could sense an independency and afraid because I had lied to my parents!)

Gradually, she started earning about Rs. 1000 per month. The earnings that she had were not enough to meet their father's medical expenses and feed all members of the family. "Un dino mujhe bahut dukh hota tha, ki main ghar mein sabse badi sadasya hone ke bawajood bhi kuch nahi kar pa rahi thi. Sirf Rs. 1000 se kuch nahi hota tha!" said Rekha while speaking to our team members. (Those days I used to feel so depressed looking at my family's conditions. Though being the eldest, I couldn't do much. What difference can Rs. 1000 make to nourish a living?)

Her life has been a path of ups and downs from a very tender age. Once on her way to a client in the nearby village, she heard of a team who was pursuing people to carry forward the art of carpet weaving. She enquired her friends and relatives about the team and the very next day, she started with her hunt. Her search ended at a temple located in her village where the team was interacting with women weavers. On introducing herself, she found that the team members were from Jaipur Rugs Foundation and their purpose of visit was to analyze the livelihoods of people in her village. They also encouraged and motivated people towards stabilized sources of income. One of which was carpet weaving. Her spirit felt the need of understanding the term and she related weaving with stitching while interacting with the team members.

"Kaleen bhunai ka jab meine suna toh laga ki kuch alag baat to hai. Idhar udhar dhakhe khane se toh acha hai ki ghar bait kar hi kaam kiya jaye," Rekha told to one of us. (Having heard of carpet weaving, I thought this art is very different. Rather than wandering places, I thought why not work while sitting at home?).

After knowing about carpet weaving training, its benefits and consequences, Rekha discussed the opportunity with her parents. At first there was a resistance from her mother as she wasn't sure of the concept of carpet weaving. Rekha sarcastically smiled and rolled out what her mother had told her while resisting her from participating in the carpet weaving training, "Kahe ko bawli banti hai. Kyu aur kaam leti hai aur patanahi kese log hai. Joh tumhare pankh nikal rahe hai woh kabhi kat jayenge!" (Why do you want to be stupid. Why do you want to take more work and we do not how these people are? The wings on which you want to fly will get damaged someday).

The foundation's team members, Rekha and her friends managed to somehow convince her parents. They were convinced on the fact that Rekha does not have to travel to other places to earn a substantial living and that other female weavers will also be working with her. The training that was conducted by the foundation, focused on different types of knots, carpet designing, reading maps etc. The program also focused on health, gender and sensitivity issues. "Aap ki team bahut acha sikhati hai. Muje khushi hui yeh jaan ke ki Kaleen bhunai ki vajah se hum kafi haad tak acha paisa kama lete hai. Aur doosri mude par bhi baat cheet karne se yeh mehsoos hua ki aage aur kya ho sakta hai," Rekha said. (Your team was supportive and teaches well. I am pleased to learn that through carpet weaving we can earn a good amount in our family. Having interacted on various issues I felt that there is a lot to be explored in future!)

Rekha, having finished with her carpet weaving training, started as a weaver. A loom was installed by the foundation at her neighbour's house where she started with her career. With experience, her speed of weaving carpets increased. Impressed by her performance and production levels in a span of 12 months, seniors at the field recommended her to the next level. She became a master trainer at the age of 18 and trained at least 16 other young female weavers in her village.

Thinking about her constant struggle in convincing her conservative parents, she today feels proud of her fight. Having worked for three years in carpet weaving, she said, "Aaj mein kafi ladkiyo ko sikha deti hu. Acha lagta hai. Meri maa bhi khush hoti hai aur baapu kehte hai ki mein teacherni hu! Unko acha lagta hai jaati biraadri mein mere bare mein baat karna! Aaj lagta hai ki mein badi ho gayi hu. Mujhe pata hai ki aage mein kaha tak jaana chaungi" (Today I am teaching many female weavers. I feel good about it. My mother is extremely overwhelmed and my father says that I am a good teacher. They feel proud about my achievements and speak a lot about me in community meetings. Today, I feel that I have grown up. I have a sense of future and know where it is heading towards)

Today, she earns Rs. 3500 – Rs. 4000 per month and is very much committed towards her work. Her brother is pursuing a computer course for a better job. Her father's condition is better and is working efficiently in Jaipur. It is because of her earnings that her two young brothers are receiving education.

Rekha (Master Trainer) working with the trainees.

"Acha toh lagta hai ki main khud kama leti hu aur apne pairo par khadi hu. Lekin mein sari pagaar maa ko de deti hoon. Ab woh Bhaiya ko pese dedi hai computer course ke liye. Kabhi muje lagta hai ki maa jitna bhaiya ke bare mein sochti hai, kya meri shikhsha ke bare mein bhi sochti hai kya?"(I feel good about my earnings and I am able to stand on my own. I give my salary to my mother who then gives fees to my brothers for their education. Sometimes I wonder if my mother thought of my education as much as she think of my brother), Rekha said.

As she reads out the design map in her boli and instructing other women weavers, she looks very much immersed yet very ambitious to conquer anything that comes in her way. She is engaged to a college fresher in Sikar and will be soon getting married to him. When asked what would have been another alternative for her if it wasn't for carpet weaving, she smiled and replied: "Main aap jaisi bana chahti thi" (I wanted to be like you!)

■ The Question of Gender Equality!

Name: Sanju Kanwar

Occupation: Carpet weaver

I used to read in books – how Cinderella was trapped in her house with her step sisters and mother. I used to wonder if she never felt the desire of being free. Though this is a fairy tale, yet the story implies to real life situations. Girls of my community are like the character – Cinderella, trapped in their own house, trapped because of their ideal images imposed by the societies.

I hail from a Rajput community – a very conservative section where women and females especially are not allowed to speak for their rights. The men of this community are the only decision makers, so what if a male is your younger brother or youngest son! If there is a male in the house, he is the sole decision – maker of everything.

I am 18 years old, an adult as per the constitution, yet not independent to take decisions on my own. I pursued my studies till eight standard in a nearby school. I had big dreams and fantasies to finish my schooling and to pursue higher studies. I was 14 then and my favourite subjects were Social Studies, Science, English and Maths. When I topped my eight standard results, my mother was extremely pleased. She was so overwhelmed that she distributed sweets at every corner of our village (Abrasar, a village in Churu). She said, "Aaaj tune meri bhi tamana puri kardi!" (you fulfilled my desire too!).

That very day, my father returned from his work late in the evening. I could still sense my mother's excitement. She cooked puris, kheer and bhujiyas on the occasion. When my father asked her what was so special about the day, she excitedly exclaimed, "Bitto ne top kiya hai class mein! Isne apne ghar ka naam bahut roshan kiya hai!" My father was happy on hearing this news. He called me and said that he was a proud father. We had our dinner following which I started to get ready for the very next day. I was packing my bags when I could hear loud noises. I came out of my room to check if there was a fight in the neighborhood but the noises were coming from my parent's room. I went near to the door and could hear their voices clearly. My father said, "Toh kya hua ki usne top karliya. Hai toh Ladki jaat. Mein kaha tak padaunga usko. Gav mein toh barvi ke liye school bhi nahi. Phir itni pad-likh kar kya karna hai. Shaadi hokar toh ghar hi sambhaal na hai" (So what if she has topped her class. She is a girl. Till what level I need to invest her studies? We don't have proper schools in our village too. And what will she do after studying. After marriage, she will be required to do the household work.)

I could sense my mother's tears. She stood for me before him. She wanted to fulfill my desire of studying more. But with hers I could see my dreams sulking too. I could then hear some foot steps coming towards the door. I ran towards my room, thinking of what to do next. I pretended as though I was busy reading a book. My father had come out of his room, looking for me. When he saw me with all the books around, he came in. He smiled and said, "Ab padai bahut hogayi….ghar ke kaam-kaaz bhi seekh le!" (Enough of studies now..learn how to take care of household and groceries). I just looked into his eyes with tears and I could sense he felt the same. He then said, "Main agar tuje padaounga toh parivaar bhukha mar jayega.. aur agar tu ladka hoti toh yeh sab mein nahi sochta.." (If I invest in your studies, our family will be living in hunger. If you were a boy, things would have been different!)

I kept quiet and just nodded my head. There was nothing in my defense to say. The whole night I was awake. Thoughts preoccupied my mind and I kept asking myself why is there so much of differentiation between a male and a female?. Though in this nation, we worship goddesses and consider females to be a re-born version of the goddesses, yet we are considered worthless to be invested upon! I knew it was a tough job convincing my father. My mother had tried her best but the very next day, she was all fine with not letting me go to pursue education further. For many days, I tried convincing my mother. Many a times it so happened that on seeing other children going to school, my heart sulked deep inside. Even my teacher visited our home and talked to my parents, but there was no turning back from the decision once taken.

My father is a farmer and occasionally gets a lump sum at home. Survived by three sisters and a younger brother, our family income those days, were very less to feed us all and take care of our basic amenities. I had left schooling but the fire of reading and knowing more couldn't fade off.

One day on my way to a friend's house, I saw a group of people talking to women in our neighbourhood. The group seemed well-organized and educated.

On joining the discussion, I realized that they were from a foundation who wanted to empower women through carpet weaving. They were collecting names of women who would like to earn a better living. Without giving any second thoughts, I added my name to the list. On returning home, my mother asked me whole sorts of questions on such people and whether I knew them or if I had met them. My younger cousin had told her that I was participating in a meeting like this. So the outburst, was natural!

In the evening, ladies from our neighbourhood were talking about carpet weaving to my mother as well. She thought of joining the group as well since she felt that this would raise our family income. She asked me if I had registered, to which I said yes. The very next day, I and my mother searched for such group and on meeting them they managed to convince us about carpet weaving. The search ended here, however the fear crept in both of us. We were scared of facing my father. Late at night, after dinner my mother and I took the courage of asking him to allow us joining carpet weaving training. He first replied, "Mein mard hu…humare ghar ki aurto ko koi hak nahi banta kamaane ka jab tak mein zinda hu!" (I am a man…my family's women or ladies do not have the rights to earn a living until I am alive!).

I could feel my sweat pouring at the base of my spine. My mother explained him the training process, about those people and the need of doing so. For a week, I and my mother constantly pricked him with new ideas and thinking with a broad mindset. One fine day, we insisted him to meet one of the trainers from foundation. After a detailed lecture on what we will be trained on and how is carpet weaving useful, the trainer somehow managed to get my father in a convincing mode.

A few more girls from my village had a similar problem. Yet the foundation members (Jaipur Rugs Foundation), could easily convince the lot as it didn't involve the risk of earning outside homes and villages. The members told us that we will be provided with looms at our homes and a master trainer to train us on carpet weaving. My mother had known this art since her childhood but after having married to my father, she had left carpet weaving.

Very soon, we started with our carpet weaving training with the foundation. There were experts from different places like Uttar Pradesh, West Bengal etc. to teach us the skills. My mother could pursue much of the training as it was getting hectic for her to manage everything at home but I still continued learning. In a period of six months, I finished the training and then a loom was installed at my house where we started weaving our first carpet. Friends and girls aged 16-17 years came down at my house to weave. The group was made by the foundation and we followed the instructions religiously. Finally, our first carpet was made and it was now the time for our salaries.

The day I received my first salary, I felt proud of it. I could sense power defining me, my ambitions and my confidence increased. When I showed this to my father, he felt overwhelmed! I gave have of the amount to him and half to my mother for household groceries. They looked at me with pride and couldn't stop adoring me!

Today, it has been a year and a half since I have been working as a carpet weaver. And this has changed my life drastically. Until now I always overheard people saying how money enhances one's persona of living. And it is indeed true. I started with Rs. 2000 per month and now I earn Rs. 4000 per month. I give half of my earnings to my parents and the rest I save in a bank! Still I wish if I could get an opportunity to study further. Had I had the chance of going to a college, I would have earned even better.

■ Life is a Matter of Holding on...

Name: Puja and Manju Singh

Occupation: Carpet Weavers

Puja and Manju, unlike other girls of their age have seen it all in their lives. Aged 16 and 17 years respectively, these girls are sharing the responsibility of their family. Survived by parents and three siblings, these young ladies are striving hard in the battle to earn sustainable living.

Located in Ambarsar village in Churu, their father Gulab Singh, aged 45 years earns a living by selling wheat from nearby farms. He earns Rs. 50 per day, an amount insufficient to meet the daily needs of the family. The expenses of the family coughed up when the doctors declared that Puja's mother is suffering from Tuberculosis.

On being visited by JRF's team, Gulab Singh said, "Family planning bahut zaroori hai. Itne logo ka palan poshan, mere jaisa gareeb nahi kar sakta!" (Family planning is very vital. To feed so many family members is impossible for a beggar like me!)

Manju, the eldest daughter pursued her education till fifth standard in a nearby school in the village. When asked on whether it was her decision to do so, she softly replied, "Amma ki tabiyat bahut biggade jaa rahi thi. Main agar school jaati thi toh ghar par koi nahi sambhal pata tha. Isiliye padai chod di!" (My mother was falling severely ill every day. If I went to school, there was no one to take good care of her. That's why I had to leave my education!)

Having said these words she shyed away from talking further. Then we asked Puja if she would like to continue with her studies, to which she replied, "Pad loongi par didi ki madad kaun karega?" (I can study but who will help my sister!)

Gulab Singh in the month of August had met with a frightful accident. On falling from a five storey building while helping construction workers, he fractured both his ankles. His medical expenses shot up to more than a lakh. "Mujhe toh ab upar wala hi bacha sakta hai. Mein kahan jaun. Jeene ka koi matlab nahi hai" (Only God can save me from these hurdles. Where do I go? It is no use to be alive!) said Gulab Singh.

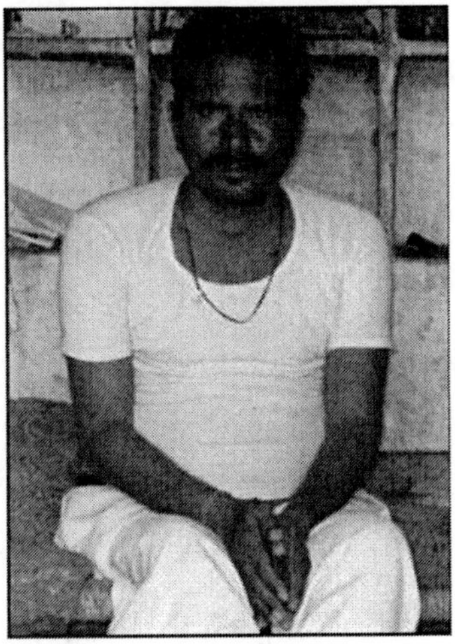

Gulab Singh thinking hard to survive in future

Two years ago, Gulab Singh had heard of Jaipur Rugs Foundation implementing looms in village households. Somehow, he attended the social meetings organized by the foundation and got convinced on having a loom installed at his home. He had attended the weaving skill training and along with the neighbourhood, he started to weave carpet on a part-time basis to earn a better living. Subsequently after a year, Puja and Manju learnt carpet weaving skills and they started earning while sitting at homes.

"Muje acha lag raha hai jab mein paise kama rahi hu. Kam se ka amma ki davaiyo ka kharcha toh nikal jata hai!" said Manju when asked on her experience in carpet weaving (I like the fact that I am earning money now. At least medical expenses of my mother can be met through such earnings!). At present she alone earns Rs. 4000 per month to take care of her family needs. Her parents are ill and she along with Puja takes the charge of the family. "Main bhi kaleen ki bhunai karke didi ki madad kar deti hu! Acha bahut lagta hai jab do hazaar rupaiy haath mein aate hai. Ise main kharch nahi karti hu!" said Puja on being asked if she helps her sister in carpet weaving. (I help my elder sister in weaving a carpet. It feels good when I get paid Rs. 2000 for the art. I do not spend this amount anywhere!).

While taking a leave from Gulab Singh's house after meeting the girls and the family, Gulab Singh replied, "Yeh toh loom hai madamji jiski vajah se mein aur mera parivaar zinda hai. Nahi toh main kab ka khatam ho jaata!" (It is only because of this loom madam that I and my family could survive otherwise I was finished!)

* * *

Gita with her daughter Manju.

Name: Gita

Occupation: Carpet Weaver

Age: 35 years

Work Experience: One year

Family Status: Poor

Village: Ambrasar (Churu)

Community: OBC

Survived by five children and a husband, Gita started carpet weaving a year ago. She works on a part-time basis since their main source of earnings is cattle raising and farming. She was hardly educated and got married at a very early age. Since then she engaged herself in cattle raising while her husband sold the produce from their farm. Having given birth to three daughters and two sons, Gita decided to let her eldest daughter study in the village school. For her academics fee, they sold their land in fragments and Gita adopted carpet weaving on a part time basis. "Mujhe apni beti ki fikar hai ki kahin who meri tera na rehjaye! Usse pad likh kar bada aadmi ban na hai" (I am worried about my daughter. I hope she doesn't stay like me. She needs to study well and become a better person).

Manju, Gita's eldest daughter is 15 years old and assists her mother in carpet weaving whenever she comes back from school. On a part time basis Gita earns at a max of Rs. 1200 per month while her husband is able to collect Rs. 30 per day.

❑❑❑

Select References

A.C. Nielson (2005), *Global Online Survey on Consumer Opinions.*

AICTE, *Committee on Technical Education for Real India*, Panel Report, 1996.

All India Management Association (AIMA) (1984), FORE Study on Effective Management, *Indian Management*, April 1984.

A.P.J. Abdul Kalam, *Integrated Partnership for Development*, Republic Day Address, 2005.

Baha'I International Community (2005), *Principles of Development: Spirituality Based Indicators.*

Bhargava, Shivganesh (2003), *Transformational Leadership: Value Based Management for Indian Organisations*, Response Books.

Bhaumik Mani (2004), Answers in the Mystic's Lab, *The Best of Speaking Tree*, The Times of India, Vol. II, 2004.

— (2008), The Cosmic Detective, Penguin.

Brown, Ian (1999), Management Theory/From the Scriptures, several articles in *The Hindu*, 1999.

Byrone, Rhonda (2007), *The Secret*, Simon & Schuster.

Capra Fritzof (1973), *The Tao of Physics*, Bantam Books, New York.

Chakraborty, S.K. (1976), *MBO: An Integrated Approach*, Macmillan.

— (1987), *Managerial Effectiveness and Quality of Work Life*, Tata McGrawHill.

— (1993), *Managerial Transformation by Values: A Corporate Pilgrimage*, Sage Publications.

— (1991), *Management by Values: Towards Cultural Congruence*, Oxford University Press.

— (1995), *Human Values for Managers*, Wheeler.

— (2004), *The Management and Ethics Omnibus*, Oxford University Press.

Chadha, Prem (2007), *The Orderly Workplace: An Exploration into Holistically Disciplined Worklife*, Macmillan.

Chowdhry, Kamla (1999), The Spiritual Path to Development, *The Hindu*, August 1, 1999

Canadian Industrial Development Agency (CIDA) (1991), *Sustainable Development: (Discussion Paper), July 1991.*

Csikszent, Mihaly (1991), *Flow: The Psychology of Optimal Experience*, Harpercollins.

DeBono, Edward (1999), *Six Thinking Hats* (Revised and updated) Penguin.

Department of Management Studies (DOMS), Workshop on *Maternalistic Style of Management: An Indian Perspective*, Kodaikanal, April 6-8, 1988.

Diwakar, R.R. (1986), *The Science of Human Values, The Hindu*, June 17th, 1986.

Drucker, Peter (1954), *The Practice of Management*, New York: Harper.

— (1954), *Management: Tasks, Responsibilities, Practices*, Heinemann.

Ed. Cohen (2007), *Leadership without Border – Successful Strategies from World Class Leaders*, Wiley India.

Executive Access Survey on *What Demotivates Employees at Workplace?*, 2006.

Fukuyama, Francis (1992), *The End of History and the Last Man*, Free Press, New York.

Ganguly R.C. (2001), *Dharmic Values and HRM*, Vikas.

Garderner, Howard (2008), *Five Minds of the Future*, HBS Press.

Gellerman, William *et al.* (1990), *Values and Ethics in Organisation and System Development (OD – HSD) (Responding to Dilemmas in Professional Life)* Jossey – Bass.

Gendlin Eugene T. (1982), *Focusing*, Bantam Books.

Ghemawat, Pankaj (2007), *Redefining Global Strategy*, HBS Press.

Ghose, Sisir Kumar (1976), *Cursed City: The Road back from Animal Farm, The Statesman*, July17/24, 1976

Ghoshal, Sumantra and Christopher A. Bartlett (1998), *The Individualized Corporation*, Random.

— (2002), *Managing Radical Change*, Penguin.

Global Forum of Spiritual Leaders and Parliamentarians, Kremlin, USSR, March, 1990.

Grant Thornton International Business Report on Small and Medium Sized Business Leaders, 2007.

Gupta, K.M. (2004), The Ultimate Holy Book of Humanity, *The Best of Speaking Tree, The Times of India*, Vol. II, 2004.

Handy, Charles (1995), *Gods of Management*, Random.

Humble John (1973), *How to Manage by Objectives*, Amacom.

ITC, Chairman Emeritus, A.N. Haksar, *Speech at AGM*, 1985

ITC Chairman's Speech: *Vision, Values and Vitality: Pillars of Transformation*, AGM, 2006

Izzo, John (2008), *The Five Secrets You must Discover before you Die*, Berrett-Koehler Publishers.

Kakkattuthadathil Tomy Paul (2001), *Otherness and Being Oneself* (Thinking with Martin Buber on Interconnectivity and Personal identity), New Delhi, Intellectual Publications.

Kerr, Clark *et al.* (1964), *Industrialism and Industrial Man* (Second Edition), New York: OUP.

Knowling, Jr., Robert E. (2002), Leading with Vision, Strategy and Values, in Hasselbein, Frances, *et al.* (edi.), *Leading for Innovation and Organising for Results* (The Drucker Foundation, Wisdom to Action Series), Jossey-Bass, 2002.

Kumar, Nirmalya (2009), *India's Global Powerhouses*.

— (2009b), *Global Powerhouses made in India, Sunday Times of India*, April 5, 2009.

Lok Sabha (Golden Jubilee of Independence) Resolution (1997) on Agenda for India, September 1997.

Madan, C., C. Cangan, G.P. Rao (edi) (1998), *HRD: Value Based Management*, Jaipur.

Mali, Paul (1986), *MBO Updated: A Handbook of Practices and Technich's for MBO*, John Wiley.

McGaw, Nancy and Lisa Fabish (2006), *Put Your Values to Work*, Harvard Management Review Update, 2006.

McLuham, Marshal and Bruce R. Powers (1989), *The Global Village* (Transformation in World life and Media in the 21st Century), Oxford University Press.

McCormak, Mark (1997), *The Value of Values, Business Today*, Nov. 7-21, 1997.

Ministry of Education, Government of India (1985), *Challenge of Education: A Policy Perspective*, 1985.

Maira Arun, and Peter Scot (1997), *The Accelerating Organisation: Embracing the Human Face of Change*, McGrawHill.

Misra, Narayanji (2008), *Better Management and Effective Leadership through the Indian Scriptures*, Delhi: Pustak Mahal.

Rev. Mary (2007), *Importance of Balance, The Sunday Times*, May 13, 2007.

Mother Teresa (1979), Managers Must Remember, Calcutta Management Association (CMA) Newsletter: *The Manager*, Oct. 1979.

Murthy, N.R. Narayana (2008), *Driven by Values* (Interview, ISB Insight, September, 2008).

— (2009), *A Better India, A Better World*, Penguin Books.

Naisbitt, John (200), *HiTech HiTouch: Technology and our search for meaning, Nicholas Brearey.*

NFL MBL India Ltd. (2002), *Survey of Indian Corporate Executives.*

Nicholson Nigel (2006), *Managing the Human Animal.*

Nilekani, Nandan (2008), *Imaging India: Ideas for the New Century*, Penguin.

Outlook Business, *Special Issue on Global India's True Multinationals*, February 2008

Pareek, Udai, *Beyond Management* (Essay in the process of Institution Building), New Delhi, Oxford, 1981.

Pandit, Sreenivas (2001), *Thought Leaders*, Tata McGrawHill.

Prahalad, C.K. (2004), *Fortune at the bottom of the Pyramid*, Wharton School Publishing .

Price Waterhouse (1998), *Straight from the CEO*, Nicholas Brearey.

Pruzan, Peter (1998), *From Control to Value Based Management and Accountability* in Journal of Business Ethics, Vol. 17, 1379-1394, 1998.

Pruzan, Peter *et al.* (2007), *Leading with Wisdom: Spiritual Based Leadership in Business*, Greenleaf Publishing, UK.

Puckey, Walter (1967), *Organisation in Business Management; A Guide for Managers and Potential Managers*, Random House.

Radhakrishnan, S. (1997), *Search for Truth*, Hind Pocket Books.

Radhakrishnan-Swami, Meenakshi (2007), Business Standard, *What they don't teach you at B School*, Tata McGrawHill.

Ranjan, Sudhanshu (2000), Nature and the Art of Good Governance, *The Times of India* (The Speaking Tree), September 28, 2000.

Rao, G.P. (1979), *I as an attitude: Is it a deterrent to Worker Participation in Management?*, Panjab University (PU) Management Review, Jan.–June 1979.

— (1981), *Maternalistic management needed, The Hindu*, August 4, 1981. (Reprinted, among others, Aurobindo Action, September 1981).

— (1982), Cautious Note on Motivation, *The Financial Express*, July 31, 1982.

— (1983), *Elitism: Major limitation of present education system, The Hindu*, September 12, 1983.

— (1989), Management Education in India: A Proposal in Philip J. and D. Shanker Narayan (edi.), *Management Education in India*, Bangalore: IIM.

— (1990), Network cooperation for institution building: An experience, Association of Management Institutions in South Asia (AMDISA), *First Academic CMIC Conference*, Hyderabad, 1990.

— (1990b), Work Ethics, Work ethic and Indian Psycho-Philosophy: Some ideas on a Maternalistic model in Chakraborty, S.K. (edi.), *Human Response Development: Exploring Transformational Values*, New Delhi: Wiley Eastern..

— (1991), Interpersonal Effectiveness in Suryanarana, C. (edi.), *Contemporary Studies in Organisational Behaviour*, New Delhi: Discovery.

— (1991b), *Manager as Karma Yogi, ibid.*

— (1992), *Management Philosophy: Indian Perspective, Indian Management* (AIMA), February, 1992.

— (1993), *The purpose of a professional's life: A study of perceptions by management students* in Rastogi, J.L. and Bidhi Chand (edi.) *Management and Business Education in India* (Essays in honour of Prof. T.N. Kapoor).

— (1996), *Human Values in Industrial Organisations: Feminine Perspective* (IIMC: MCHV Research Monograph), Sage.

— (1997), *Human Values in Management: Feminine Perspective, Indian Management* (AIMA), August 1997.

— (1998), *An odyssey of self discovery, The Hindu*, May 5, 1998.

— (2001), Institution Building with Innovation and Indigenous Values Orientation: An Odyssey by The Indian Institute of Plantation Management, Banagalore, Bangalore University, Bangalore, *Conference on Management Education.*

— (2002), *Spandan and the integral development of the human person: India insights, experiences and experiments*, Journal of Human Values (IIMC-MCHV), 8:2, January–July 2002.

Reputation Institute, USA, Global 2000, *The World's Best Corporate Reputations*, 2008.

Rokeach, M. (1973), *The Nature of Human Values*, New York, The Free Press.

Saxena, A.P. (2008), *Jawaharlal Nehru: The Spirit of Humanism*, Ane Books.

Secretan, Lance H.K. (1996), *Reclaiming Higher Ground*, Response.

Seng Peter M. (1990), *The Fifth Discipline: The Art and Practice of the Learning Organisation*, Doubleday Currency.

Sharma, Subhash (1996), *Management in New Age: Western Windows, Eastern Doors*, New Age International.

— (2007), *New Mantras in Corporate Corridors from Ancient Roots to Global Routes*, New Age International.

Singh, Balmiki Prasad (2008), *Bahudha and The Post 9/11 World.*

Singh, Karan (2004), *Symbiosis between Science and Spirit, The Best of Speaking Tree*, (TOI), Vol. II, 2004.

Spandan IBA Award on Human Values for Professionals, 2007 and 2008, Nomination presentations.

Spandan IMI Seminar on Value based Management, Feb. 2006.

Sri Aurobindo Ashram, Auroville, Pondicherry (1990), *Mother's Ministry of Management.*

— (1998), *Powers Within* (Selections from the Works of Swami Aurobindo and the Mother).

Srinivas, Kalburgi, *Human Values and Organisational Effectiveness*, Madan, C. et al. (edi.), HRD; *Value Based Management*, 1998.

Swami Sukhabodhananda, (2007), *Have faith in yourself*, *The Times of India*, January 8th, 2007.

— (2008), *Life is just a Process of Transformation*, *The Times of India* (The Speaking Tree), December 5, 2008.

Torre, Joseph M. De (1989), *The Humanism of Modern Philosophy*, Center for Research and Communication, College of Arts and Sciences (Metro Manila, Philippines).

— (1995), *Generation and Degeneration: A Survey of Ideologies, Southeast Asian Science Foundation*, Inc. (Philippines).

Tracy, Brian (2002), *Eat That Frog*, Berrett-Koehler Publishers.

Theo, Phil, Marguilite (1998), *Tracing the cyclic rhythm of opposites*, *The Times of India* (Speaking Tree), July 18th, 1998.

— (1999), *The Yin and Yong of the body and the mind*, *The Times of India* (Speaking Tree), November 29, 1999.

— (2000), *The Fabric of Creation Essence and its Echo*, *The Times of India*, (Speaking Tree), August 11th, 2000.

UN Fiftieth Anniversary, October 1995.

UN Global Compact 2000, Task Force of Academic Community on developing a set of Principles for Responsible Business Education, 2007.

Venkatesan, R. (2004), *Spiritual Quotient Leverages of IQ and EQ*, The Best of Speaking Tree, (TOI), Vol. II, 2004.

Wakhloo, Arun (1999), *Managing from the Heart: Unfolding Spirit in People and Organisation*, Response Books.

Wilson, Edward O. (1975), *Sociobiology: The New Synthesis*. Belknap Press, 1975

— (1979) *On Human Nature*. Harvard University Press.

— (1994), Naturalist, Shearwater Books.

Yergin, Daniel and Joseph Stainslaw (2002), *The Commanding Heights*, Free Press.

❑❑❑